Pitt Press Series

P. TERENTI

PHORMIO

This edition can be obtained with or without vocabulary

P. TERENTI
PHORMIO

EDITED BY

JOHN SARGEAUNT, M.A.

ASSISTANT MASTER AT WESTMINSTER

Cambridge:
at the University Press
1914

CAMBRIDGE
UNIVERSITY PRESS

University Printing House, Cambridge CB2 8BS, United Kingdom

Cambridge University Press is part of the University of Cambridge.

It furthers the University's mission by disseminating knowledge in the pursuit of education, learning and research at the highest international levels of excellence.

www.cambridge.org
Information on this title: www.cambridge.org/9781107487215

First published 1914
First paperback edition 2015

A catalogue record for this publication is available from the British Library

ISBN 978-1-107-48721-5 Paperback

PREFACE

WHEN a word or a phrase which calls for a note occurs more than once in the play, the references are given on its first occurrence but the later passages are as a rule not annotated.

It may seem that a vocabulary is out of place even in an elementary edition of a play of Terence. It is however a saving of time, especially for those who begin Latin somewhat late. In default of corrected editions of the current lexicons, vocabularies may have a use of their own. Thus the lexicons fail to give the only meaning which *multimodis* bears in the comedians, whatever meaning it may have in Lucretius. There are also many words of which the most usual meanings are not those which appear to be most familiar to the beginner. Familiar examples are *peto*, *perdo*, *nanciscor*, and *incipio*. More distinct errors are found in the meanings usually assigned to *gurges* and *silex*. Plants have suffered a good deal, as when the foxglove is turned into a native of Italy or parsley is desired to grow in a wet ditch.

Sometimes the lexicons allow too wide a range, as when it is implied that *indoles* can be used of a man of mature years or that *mox* means 'soon' elsewhere than in the phrase *quam mox*. In other cases the opposite error occurs, as when *interea* is denied its common meaning of 'anon' or 'after a time.' It seems then that the vocabularist may make himself useful. His two drawbacks are that his account of a word is necessarily meagre and that, like his predecessors, he himself may be liable to err.

J. S.

WESTMINSTER, 1914.

INTRODUCTION

THE comedies of Terence are the work of a man who, though he had no Roman, probably not even any European, blood, was a master of the Latin tongue. They thus belong to the language of Rome, but they are in no sense a representation of Roman life. They are in origin Greek plays, but they belong to Latin literature, for to the Roman even the closest translation from Greek was none the less a Latin work. Yet they stand apart from Latin literature because all else that was great in Latin literature, based though it was upon Greek, had something of substance and of feeling that was essentially its own. They stand apart from Roman life because the characters are Athenians, of an epoch that showed but little likeness to anything that was Roman. Yet they have a link with Roman life because they reflect the desire of a school of young Romans to shape their literature after the models of Athens. Our own language possesses many translations from the literatures of other nations and other times, but none that were undertaken quite in the spirit of Terence or of those who set Terence to work and probably assisted him in his labours.

The Greek originals of these plays were written in the late fourth and early third centuries before Christ. What changes Terence made we cannot exactly say. It is probable that the lines, as actors call them, were somewhat close translations, though the work is so well done that this probability cannot be inferred from the style and language of the plays. Plautus, who had preceded Terence in the transplantation of these comedies, dealt more freely with his originals. His scenes and his characters were still supposed to be Greek, but he surrounded them with a new atmosphere and did not shrink from allusions to Italian life and politics and thought. The works of Menander and Apollodorus and Diphilus thus got a new setting. To Terence and to the Roman school of which he was the mouthpiece this free handling appeared as false art. The only liberty which they would allow themselves was the blending of two plays into one with adaptations and omissions as might be necessarily involved.

The scene of the original plays was usually, though not always, laid at Athens. The life which they present is that of a noble and wealthy class, hardly stirred to high aspirations, hardly vext by obstinate questionings, and ready to believe that the life which it has inherited, though like all lives it has its troubles, offers all that can be required for the satisfaction of the soul. The other characters, the slave, the adventurer, the courtesan, figure as accessories of this life. The comedian could not exclude them and certainly had no wish to exclude them, from his scene. They were necessary for the comedy of situation and intrigue. It cannot be said that a young Athenian gentleman was above deceiving his father, even though he sometimes felt compunction for his deceit, but his line of deception was not clever enough and not whole-hearted enough to amuse the audience. And further the more vulgar characters were required as contrasts to these same young Athenian gentlemen, who were mostly of one mould, and to the three or four types into which in old Athenian gentlemen these differences had developed. The slave was often and the adventurer was necessarily clever, and cleverness seems not to have been a quality that could be laid at the door of a young Athenian gentleman of this epoch. There were still quick wits at Athens else these plays could not have been either written or appreciated, but quick wits must have been rare in the class with which the plays deal. To the young nobleman years might bring experience, but years could not create ability, and the intelligence of a middle-aged Athenian nobleman hardly went beyond the lines of common-sense. Like old Capulet he could keep his estate together, but his brains, like old Capulet's, were in many cases not fit for much more. It was perhaps well that your Antipho lackėd alike the daring and the passion of a Romeo and that your Phanium was still more unlike a Juliet. Our comedians might else have found material for tragedies, and for tragedy their turn of mind was hardly fit.

If tragedy was out of their line, at any rate Menander and Apollodorus saw well enough the humours of Athenian life. Whether they saw its vanity is another question. If they did, their plays might be accounted grim satires on an age, or at least on a class, which had ceased to look upward, ceased to look forward, and cared for little but a material comfort which proved impossible to secure. The young man obtains the bride of his heart and expects to live happily ever afterward : the old man looks at his wife and wishes the hag were in her grave. He ascribes her faults to the weakness and folly of woman and does not see (as how should he see?) that his own lack of ideals has made her what she is. Such a life gives the comedian no characters that we can take to our hearts. Menander could no more give us a Benedick or a Beatrice than he could give us a Hamlet. A play that were all Polonius and Laertes could not be a work of the highest genius. A play that were all Sir Anthony and Captain Absolute needs for its success more pure wit than was possest by these dramatists of Athens.

How is it then that these plays still attract and amuse us, still allow even inexperienced actors to hold an audience from the first line to the last? Perhaps one answer might be that, however poor may have been the life which they present, they are at any rate skilful presentations of its sentimental side. The life was not exactly such as they show it, and yet there is the supreme quality of exactness in the dramatists' work. That exactness consists in the perfect adaptation of the means to the end. The comedians had caught the true manner of their themes, and of that manner the Roman translator or adapter lost nothing. The big bow-wow manner, which Scott claimed to possess, has its place in comedy as in other forms of fiction, but not in such comedy as deals with beings of this Athenian type. Scott admitted that for such a world the manner of Jane Austen far excelled his own. There are forms of life in Jane Austen's novels which surpass the life of Antipho and Chremes, but there are also forms of life which may well be compared with it. While her novels were in the writing, great deeds were doing, great men were showing their greatness. Yet how little we hear of the great deeds and the great men, and how few of her characters seem to have any care for either. Nevertheless we know well enough that in the country at the time there were many men and women who cared much for both. There are passages in the novels, especially in *Persuasion*, which show that Jane Austen herself was one of these. If Sir Walter Elliot thought of little but good looks, his daughter knew of the services of Admiral Croft long before she expected to meet that gallant sailor in the flesh. A modern novel will supply us with another illustration. We may perhaps be justified in inferring from the character of the Baron in *The Caravaners* that there is in one part of Germany a class none too strong in the brain and none too sound in the heart. None the less we know that the Baron is no type of the true German. There are other classes in Germany who may well claim our respect and something more. Jane Austen's pages are less one-sided than either Menander's plays or the Countess von Arnim's novel. She can show us men and women who win not only our respect but our affection. She portrays beings who know how to lead rational lives and to make something, if not the best, of the faculties that are in them. On the other hand she shows us a crowd of which this cannot be said. In these plays there are persons entitled to some respect but very few to claim our love. Now as no one could wish the manner of Jane Austen in her dialogues to be other than it is, so could no one desire for the purpose of these comedies a better manner than we find in Terence. The scene between Elinor and Marianne Dashwood in the twenty-ninth chapter of *Sense and Sensibility* can hardly fail to remind the reader of the relations between Antipho and

Phaedria in this play. There are indeed trifling coincidences of phrase. 'O fortunatissume Antipho,' says Phaedria, and is answered with a bitter 'Egone?' 'Happy, happy Elinor!' says Marianne, and is answered, 'Do you call me happy?' But the very resemblance serves to point the contrast. Jane Austen cared for situation and incident only so far as they threw light upon character. Our dramatists cared much less for character than for situation and intrigue. Macaulay speaks of Jane Austen's delicate touches, eluding analysis and defying the powers of description, by which she discriminates men of an ordinary type who in rank, education, and circumstances are all alike. Such delicacy of delineation was beyond the scope, perhaps beyond the power, of these dramatists. They can indeed draw characters on broad lines. The resolute old man is well contrasted with his less courageous brother. The resource and astuteness of the slave differ from the resource and astuteness of the adventurer. But the turn of the phrase is often such as either the one or the other might use. In fact the phrase is not always true to life. There is a clearness and a finish which in actual life some of the persons could not come near. But the clearness, even when it is not quite dramatic, does not offend any more than the wit which Sheridan puts into the mouth of his clodhopping squire. It brings out the situation even when it does not bring out the character. There is a far deeper and in essence more dramatic power in the less lucid comedies of Shakespeare, but the very depth of thought almost demands that we should pause and think ourselves. Menander and Apollodorus knew and Terence knew from them that no one should be compelled to pause and think even in the reading, much less in the seeing and hearing, of a comedy of intrigue.

It may be said that these limitations infringe upon the exactness which is claimed for our dramatists. The answer to such an objection must resemble the answer to another charge of improbability which may be brought against them. It must be admitted that the limitations of their stage traditions compelled them to present incidents in a form other than that in which they must have occurred. Dialogues are held in the street when they must actually have been held indoors. Men on the stage do not see each other when in life they could not have helped it. Remarks are made to an audience which is present indeed in the pit of the theatre but is not and cannot be on the pavement. A present-day playwright may choose to look upon these things as inexcusable defects. In fact we do not mind them. They do not affect the essential reality. To borrow an expression which Aristotle applied to some improbable or impossible incidents in the plot of a tragedy, we may almost claim that they are outside the drama. Though they take place before our eyes, we can accept the stage convention. The essential thing is that the things should be said. The place where they are said is not an essential part of them.

And what of Terence? Well, the fact is that we know little of Terence, and, even if we knew of him all that can be known of a man, the knowledge would have no bearing on the study of these plays. Not that we owe him little, for we owe him much. Even more, it may be, than the men whose works he borrowed, he was a master of style. They wrote the tongue of their own people. He wrote a language which in all probability was not the language of his infancy. Yet he has no cause to fear comparison. He had been a slave but he must have been one of nature's gentlemen. He was a foreigner but he spoke as a native. And he was the prince of translators. Sometimes we may fancy that we can reconstruct the original lines. The first words of this very play may perhaps have been

ὁ φίλος μάλιστα δημότης θ' οὑμὸς Γέτας.

Nevertheless the language never shows a sign of translation. It may be lawful to regret that it never occurred to Terence to put the plays into prose, but no such thought belonged to his age. It matters little, for he was such a master of his metres that the words fall into the right place and give the just emphasis. With one element in the original production the modern reader is happily not troubled. The speeches were recitative and song and the pipes sounded throughout the play. We could barely tolerate such an accompaniment to a sentimental comedy.

Terence then has done so much for us that he is entitled to a word, even though that word has no bearing on the play. He was born, we are told, at Carthage, in the year 195 B.C. His blood was Libyan or Phoenician or both, his status a slave's. His Roman master gave him an education and his freedom. That master was one of a coterie which included Polybius the historian and Panaetius the writer on morals, and looked to Scipio Aemilianus as its head. Their devotion was to Greek literature. As yet a Roman noble would hardly face the obloquy of writing under his own name. The great house of the Metelli had indeed one Saturnian line to its discredit. A generation before Terence the poet Naevius had satirized their hereditary claim to the great offices of state. It was perhaps right that their line of repartee should be prosaic, for it was a prophecy which they had the power as well as the will to carry into effect,

> Dabunt malum Metelli Naevio poetae.

The *malum* was soon interpreted, first as bonds and then as exile. Now some of the Roman nobles had learnt better things. So Terence was given his task and was allowed to confess that he had help from men who guided the policy and led the armies of the Roman people. The first of these plays, *The Lady of Andros*, appeared in 166 B.C., the other five within the next six years. Then he was sent to Greece to find fresh material, and within a twelvemonth he was dead. Men said, and other men have even been found to believe, that in those few months he translated more than a hundred comedies of Menander and his fellows. Literary gossip of a later age used to say that his manuscripts went down at sea and that he was drowned with them or died of grief for their loss. We cannot sift the gossip. All we know is that he was dead and neither then nor thereafter could Rome find a man worthy to take up his pen.

Concerning the literary powers of this comedian who thus died at the age of five and twenty there is a cryptic utterance of one who stood as high in the world of letters as in the world of action, the great Julius Caesar. Caesar misses in these plays the true force of comedy and cries to their author 'O dimidiate Menander.' What does he mean? If a man faithfully translated his original, how could he be described as that original halved? If he combined two plays into one, as Shakespeare blent the caskets with the pound of flesh, still how could he be that original halved? and what does halved mean? Is Menander cleft from head to foot that his right or left half may be Terence, somewhat as Heath's caricature shows us the Duke of Wellington with his right half drest as a Field Marshal and his left as a Minister of State? From hip to hip he can scarcely be cleft, for none can say that a man's two halves are his head and his legs. And yet, however the division be made, Terence is Menander halved. We get some light on the matter from Caesar's own explanation. Terence had not the comic force of his original. Yet it cannot be doubted that the translations do not miss the comic force of the originals. Why then Menander halved? Much as Shakespeare, among the many men that he was, was two comedians, so Menander had a right half which was sentimental comedian and a left which did nothing but laugh. Sometimes a play came from one half and sometimes from the other. Terence or his friends among the great leant all to sentiment. With Caesar we may perhaps regret that some more rollicking comedy was not brought across the Ionian Sea. At the same time the full force of comedy can hardly be denied to the titular hero of the present play.

The language of Terence may for a moment seem strange to those whose Latin studies have been confined to the notebooks of a Field Marshal or the verses of a Hellenizing poet. The language of a comedian is the speech of his contemporaries. The language of Terence is the common speech of Roman gentlemen of the era when Rome had subdued Carthage and was beginning to think of wiping her out of the map. It differs from the literary language of the last century of the Republic and differs still more from the literary language of the court of Augustus. But it does not differ greatly from the language in which Cicero spoke in private and wrote to his friends. In the Augustan age the literary language had more largely coloured the speech of gentlemen. That colour spread but slowly into the countryside, and it is interesting to note that Virgil tried to give verisimilitude to his shepherds by putting into their mouths words and phrases which had once been used but had then ceased to be used in the palaces of Rome. In such matters the polite world does not always set an eternal fashion. Thus the 'quasi sex,' about six, of the Latin comedians, a use into which Cicero, the farmer's son, occasionally slipt, perhaps to the amusement of his highborn friends, is the 'quasi sei' of an Italian gentleman. In Terence the verb 'ausculto' is common enough, but soon after his time it deserted the drawing-room. Yet it remained in the kitchen and on the farm, and now as 'ascolto' is returned to the more sumptuous scene.

Of any distinction between the speech of gentle and simple Terence seems hardly to have been aware. A modern novelist or playwright will, rightly enough, make some of his characters say '*h*onour' and '*h*umour' on the one hand and ''ope' and ''ush' on the other. Terence would perhaps have accepted the opinion of his fellow-dramatist, Mr Puff, that there is no reason why the great people should have all the fine language to themselves. The slaves talk in good grammar and, if they drop some of their consonants, their masters do the same. It is to be feared that nowadays the habitual use of slang is no longer a mark of a certain class. Yet even nowadays there is at least a difference between the slang of different classes. In Terence there is of slang hardly a trace in the speech of either gentleman or servant. Why is it? It may be that the difference was less than it is in many countries to-day. Even now with all the differences between Italian dialects an Italian peasant-wife says 'Maria' as clearly as an Italian noblewoman and would fail to recognize the 'Mrier' of the East End. It may however be that our dramatists did not recognise such bad language as a legitimate source of amusement. Possibly they were more subtle than our writers of fiction, and it may not be fanciful to feel in the texture of what the slaves say an ineffable something which discriminates the expressions of thought. We cannot however say that there is such a difference of rhythm and phrase as distinguishes, for instance, the Celtic mysticism of Owen Glendower from the Norman impetuosity of Hotspur. But there were neither Hotspurs nor Glendowers in the Athens of Menander and Apollodorus.

Terence tells us that the present play is the *Epidicazomenos*, the Claimant, of Apollodorus. His accuracy here has been doubted, but, if we take his word, we may still ask who is the Claimant and what does he claim. It cannot be one who claims a girl in marriage as next of kin, because no such claim is made. An action is brought against Antipho to compel him as next of kin to marry the girl. It is true that he is not of kin at all and that the action is collusive, but still he is the defendant in the case. Phormio, an adventurer ready for any part, pretends to be a friend of the girl's deceased father and in that capacity brings an action on her behalf. He therefore is the Claimant in that he claims that Antipho shall either marry the girl or provide her with a dowry suitable to her rank in life. The patrons of Terence seem to have thought that a Roman audience would find the adventurer's name a more manageable title for the play, and a later age may well be grateful to the patrons of Terence.

It is not proposed to give the student an outline of the plot. It is clear enough and he can make it out as he goes. If he cannot, he had better abandon literature and go and dig.

May it not be added that the student of Terence should give himself the pleasure of reading *The Feast of Bacchus*, the Poet Laureate's adaptation of our author's *Self-Tormentor*?

The Metres of Terence.

The metres of these plays follow the Greek originals, with some differences made necessary by the character of the Latin language. Metres of quantity were natural in a tongue like Greek, which, though it had a pitch accent, had no perceptible stress. The Greeks continued to use them even when their accent had been changed into a stress. Ennius, who naturalized the hexameter, must have deliberately given an artificial pronunciation to many syllables of which the quantity differed in the two languages. Thus the second syllable of ἀπέκτεινα was long, and the Latin poets consequently lengthened the second syllable of *senectutem*, though in the natural speech it was short. Again, so strong was the stress on the former syllable of an iambic word that the Romans were naturally inclined to shorten the second syllable. In some words, for instance *ego*, the shortening took place so early and was so completely established that even the Hellenizing poets could not go back to the original quantity. The tendency to shorten was strongest when the iambic word was followed by a long syllable which bore the stress. Thus such a combination of words as *abi uise* was parallel with such a word as *senectutem*. In either case the Latin comedians, following the colloquial usage, shortened the second syllable. On a like principle they scanned *patĕr uenit*, and *senĕx noster*. Even when the following syllable was short we have a like scansion, as in *priŏr bibas*. It is not necessary to assume that in these cases the former of the two consonants which in poetry make the combination long is actually dropt. In vulgar speech it was doubtless often dropt, but in the comedies it is more likely to have been lightly pronounced. There was indeed one final consonant which was habitually dropt after a short vowel. This letter was *s*, and, though polite speech, under Greek influence, restored it, with the commonalty it never came back. Thus we have *minŭ' norat* and other instances in this play. A final *m* often lost its consonantal power and merely nasalized the preceding vowel. Thus we have such scansions as *nĕmpe* and *năm per eius*. In some cases *n* seems to have been in the same position as *m*, and thus we get such scansions as *ĭntelleges*. Again a double consonant was pronounced as a single consonant, and thus we have *ŏccidi* and *supĕllectile*. Last, as *mn* past to *nn* and then to *n*, we have *ŏmnium*. Such scansions as *senĕctutem* and *abĭ* are explained by what is called the law of Breves Breviantes. This name may be a sound one from the point of view of the original Indo-European language. It is however probable that in that form of the language which we call Latin the syllables in question were always short. The ancestors of the Romans spoke an unstrest language, but this was in an age of which we have no written record. The stress must have come into use before the language came to be called Latin.

The difference of quantities in Greek and Latin points to the fact that in the natural Latin, as in English, the quantities were not as well markt as in Greek. One consequence was that the Latins were not able to feel the Greek metres exactly as the Greeks felt them. The normal metre of the Greek comedy was an iambic trimeter, that is a line of three dipodies, and in the even feet restrictions were put upon the substitution of another foot for the iambus. The Latin comedians treated the line as a verse of six feet, *uersus senarius*, and allowed the same substitutions in all feet except the last. The substitutions were spondee, anapaest, dactyl, tribrach, and paraceleusmatic. On the other hand the existence of stress in Latin involved certain restrictions. Thus in a dactyl the stress must usually fall on the middle syllable, while the fifth foot could not be an iambic word, because in that case the word stress would twice running be in conflict with the verse ictus and the quantities. Exceptions to these rules are merely exceptions in appearance. Thus we have *malam crucem* at the end, but the two words had become one and were pronounced *malámcrucem*, while a preposition and a noun following were habitually pronounced as one word. The *uersus senarius* then consists of six feet, of which the last is an iambus or a pyrrhic regarded as an iambus, while each of the other feet might be an iambus or one of the substitutes for it. As a rule there is a cesura in the third, less frequently in the fourth foot.

The iambic septenarius follows, again with differences, the Greek tetrameter catalectic, and consists of seven complete and one incomplete foot. Usually it was treated as two verses, that is to say there was a diaeresis after the fourth foot, which in that case was always an iambus. When there was no diaeresis but a cesura in the fifth foot (l. 770) there might be a substitute in the fourth foot.

The iambic octonarius is the same metre except that the last foot is complete, while the iambic quaternarius is the half of the octonarius.

The trochaic septenarius followed the Greek tetrameter catalectic, consisting of seven complete and one incomplete foot. It usually had a diaeresis after the fourth foot and allowed the same substitutes as the iambic verses.

The trochaic octonarius was the same except that the last foot was complete. Shorter trochaic verses are occasionally used.

The incomplete feet with which some of these lines end are called catalectic, that is stopping short. Such feet are familiar to us, for instance,

When the | British | warrior | Queen. ||

Many lines familiar to our infancy have these catalectic feet at any place in the verse.

Ba | ba | black | sheep, ||
Have you | any | wool ? ||
Yes, | Sir, | no, | Sir, ||
Three | bags | full. ||

Here are fourteen feet of which only two are not catalectic. Such feet occur regularly in Latin lyric verse.

Nor should the substitution of an anapaest or a spondee for an iambus or other feet for a trochee present any difficulty to an

English ear. It must always be borne in mind that these Latin lines scan by quantity and not by stress, though there are certain restrictions in the matter of stress, as for instance that a dactyl must have the stress on the middle syllable in any foot of an iambic line except the first. Most English verse scans by stress, and quantity, though it has much to do with the rhythm, has nothing to do with the metre. Allowing for this difference we may compare the substituted feet in such a passage as

> There is | not wind | enough | to twirl ||
> The one | red leaf, | the last | of its clan, ||
> That dan | ces as often | as dance | it can, ||
> Hanging | so light | and hang | ing so high ||
> On the top | most twig | that looks up | to the sky. ||

Here the typical foot is represented, for instance, by 'enough,' while a metrical substitute for it, however different in rhythm, is the foot which might be spelt 'siz azaufn.'

Terence sometimes presents us with scansion which in his time was ceasing to be usual. Many verb forms had originally a long vowel before a final *t*. Later Romans seem to have found the pronunciation of a long vowel in this position to be difficult, and they habitually shortened it, except in perfects of the type of *subiit* and *petiit*. Terence sometimes keeps the quantity, as later poets occasionally did by a conventional archaism. A like ancient pronunciation appears in *aīs*. Other colloquial scansions may well have been common even in the Augustan age though they differ from the artificial use of the Hellenizing poets. Thus two vowels are often run into one, especially in dissyllables, which thus become monosyllabic. This is usual with the possessive pronouns of the singular number and with the cases of *is*. Other instances are provided by *deus*, *quoius*, *ain*, *diu*, and *eamus*. Hiatus sometimes occurs at the end of a speech and with interjections. Occasionally the long vowel of a monosyllable is shortened in hiatus, as in Virgil's *an quĭ amant*. Probably in such cases the two words were pronounced as one.

A word on elision may not be superfluous. The Romans have not left us any clear account of elision, but they have said enough to show that in most cases the elided vowel did not wholly disappear. Even without any external testimony we might be sure that such was the case. Doubtless there were instances where in rapid utterance a light vowel was not spoken, but there are sentences which a complete ignoring of the vowel would make almost unintelligible. Further the vowel is sometimes elided at the end of a speech even in cases where the second speech is not heard by the former speaker. Virgil supplies a no less crucial instance. He makes Dido end a speech with *pugnent ipsique nepotesque.* The poet resumes his narrative with an opening vowel, but he would not have commended a reader who should make his queen say *nepotesk.* In fact there are many lines of poetry which would lose their special effect if elision were the ignoring of the vowel. Musicians have compared elision to Grace notes. Certainly to an English reader elision should present no difficulties, for he is familiar with syllables which are pronounced but do not count in the scansion. Milton, who was a musician as well as a poet, knew pretty well what elision was and he used it with excellent effect. His readers do not turn 'shadow of change' into 'shad' of change,' nor should any reader commit such an outrage upon the lines of Terence or Virgil. It is best to say that elision is a literary convention and that poets have used it, as they have used other literary conventions, because it was best so to do.

CONTENTS

P. TERENTI

PHORMIO

INCIPIT TERENTI PHORMIO

ACTA LVDIS ROMANIS

L. POSTVMIO ALBINO L. CORNELIO MERVLA

AEDILIBVS CVRVLIBVS

EGERE L. AMBIVIVS TVRPIO L. ATILIVS PRAENESTINVS

MODOS FECIT FLACCVS CLAVDI

TIBIS INPARIBVS TOTA

GRAECA APOLLODORV EPIDICAZOMENOS

FACTA IIII

C. FANNIO M. VALERIO COSS

PERSONAE

PROLOGVS	
DAVOS	Servos
GETA	Servos
ANTIPHO	Adulescens
PHAEDRIA	Adulescens
DEMIPHO	Senex
PHORMIO	Parasitus
HEGIO	Aduocati
CRATINVS	Aduocati
CRITO	Aduocati
DORIO	Leno
CHREMES	Senex
SOPHRONA	Nutrix
NAVSISTRATA	Matrona

PROLOGVS

Postquám poëta uétus poëtam nón potest
Retráhere a studio et tránsdere hominem in ótium,
Maledíctis deterrére ne scribát parat;
Qui ita díctitat, quas ántehac fecit fábulas,
Tenui ésse oratióne et scripturá leui: 5
Quia núsquam insanum scrípsit adulescéntulum
Ceruám uidere fúgere et sectarí canes
Et éam plorare, oráre ut subueniát sibi.
Quod si íntellegeret, quóm stetit olím noua,
Actóris opera mágis stetisse quám sua, 10
Minus múlto audacter, quám nunc laedit, laéderet.
Nunc sí quis est, qui hoc dícat aut sic cógitet:
'Vetus sí poëta nón lacessissét prior,
Nullum ínuenire prólogum possét nouos,
Quem díceret, nisi habéret cui male díceret': 15
Is síbi responsum hoc hábeat, in medio ómnibus
Palmam ésse positam, qui ártem tractant músicam.
Ille ád famem hunc a stúdio studuit réicere:
Hic réspondere uóluit, non lacéssere.
Benedíctis si certásset, audissét bene: 20
Quod ab íllo adlatumst, síbi esse rellatúm putet.
De illó iam finem fáciam dicundí mihi,
Peccándi quom ipse dé se finem nón facit.
Nunc quíd uelim animum atténdite: adportó nouam

Epídicazomenon quám uocant comoédiam 25
Graece, Latine hic Phórmionem nóminat,
Quia prímas partis quí aget, is erit Phórmio
Parasítus, per quem rés geretur máxume,
Volúntas uostra si ád poëtam accésserit.
Date óperam, adeste aequo ánimo per siléntium, 30
Ne símili utamur fórtuna, atque usí sumus,
Quom pér tumultum nóster grex motús locost;
Quem actóris uirtus nóbis restituít locum
Bonitásque uestra adiútans atque aequánimitas.

ACTVS I

DAVOS

Servos

Amícus summus méus et popularís Geta 35
Heri ád me uenit; érat ei de ratiúncula
Iam prídem apud me rélicuom pauxíllulum
Nummórum: id ut confícerem. Confeci: ádfero.
Nam erílem filium éius duxisse aúdio
Vxórem: ei, credo, múnus hoc conráditur. 40
Quam iníque comparátumst, ei, qui mínus habent,
Vt sémper aliquid áddant ditióribus!
Quod ille únciatim uíx de demensó suo
Suóm defrudans génium conpersít miser,
Id illa úniuorsum abrípiet haud exístumans, 45
Quantó labore pártum. Porro autém Geta
Feriétur alio múnere, ubi era pépererit;
Porro aútem alio, ubi erit púero natalís dies;
Vbi ínitiabunt. Ómne hoc mater aúferet:
Puer caúsa erit mittúndi. Sed uideón Getam? 50

GETA DAVOS

Servi II

GE. Si quís me quaeret rúfus...
DA. Praestost, désine.
GE. Oh,
At ego óbuiam conábar tibi, Daue.

DA. Áccipe, em:
Lectúmst; conueniet númerus quantum débui.
GE. Amó te, et non necléxisse habeo grátiam.
DA. Praesértim ut nunc sunt móres. Adeo rés redit; 55
Si quís quid reddit, mágna habendast grátia.
Sed quíd tu es tristis?
GE. Égone? nescis quo ín metu,
Quanto ín periclo símus!
DA. Quid istuc ést?
GE. Scies,
Modo út tacere póssis.
DA. Abi, sis, ínsciens:
Quoius tú fidem in pecúnia perspéxeris, 60
Verére uerba ei crédere? ubi quid míhi lucrist
Te fállere?
GE. Ergo auscúlta.
DA. Hanc operam tíbi dico.
GE. Senis nóstri, Daue, frátrem maiorém Chremem
Nostín?
DA. Quid ni?
GE. Quid? éius gnatum Phaédriam?
DA. Tam quám te.
GE. Euenit sénibus ambobús simul, 65
Iter ílli in Lemnum ut ésset, nostro in Cíliciam
Ad hóspitem antiquom. Ís senem per epístulas
Pelléxit, modo non móntis auri póllicens.
DA. Quoi tánta erat res ét supererat?
GE. Désinas:
Sic ést ingenium.
DA. Oh, régem me esse opórtuit! 70
GE. Abéuntes ambo hic túm senes me fíliis
Relínquont quasi magístrum.

DA. O Geta, prouínciam
Cepísti duram.
GE. Mi úsus uenit, hóc scio;
Meminí relinqui mé deo irató meo.
Coepi áduorsari prímo: quid uerbís opust? 75
Sení fidelis dúm sum, scapulas pérdidi.
DA. Venére in mentem mi ístaec; namque inscítiast
Aduórsum stimulum cálces.
GE. Coepi eis ómnia
Facere, óbsequi quae uéllent.
DA. Scisti utí foro.
GE. Nostér mali nil quícquam primo; hic Phaédria 80
Contínuo quandam náctus est puéllulam
Citharístriam: hanc amáre coepit pérdite.
Ea séruiebat lénoni inpuríssumo,
Neque quód daretur quícquam; id curaránt patres.
Restábat aliud níl nisi oculos páscere, 85
Sectári, in ludum dúcere et reddúcere.
Nos ótiosi operám dabamus Phaédriae.
In quo haéc discebat lúdo, exaduorsum ílico
Tonstrína erat quaedam: híc solebamús fere
Plerúmque eam opperíri, dum inde irét domum. 90
Intérea dum sedémus illi, intéruenit
Aduléscens quidam lácrumans. Nos mirárier;
Rogámus quid sit. 'Númquam aeque' inquit 'ác modo
Paupértas mihi onus uísumst et miserum ét graue.
Modo quándam uidi uírginem hic uicíniae 95
Miserám suam matrem lámentari mórtuam;
Ea síta erat exadúorsum, neque illi béniuolus
Neque nótus neque cognátus extra unam ániculam
Quisquam áderat, qui adiutáret funus: míseritumst.

Virgo ípsa facie egrégia.' Quid uerbís opust? 100
Commórat omnes nós. Ibi continuo Ántipho
'Voltísne eamus uísere?' Alius 'cénseo:
Eámus; duc nos, sódes.' Imus, uénimus,
Vidémus. Virgo púlcra, et quo magis díceres,
Nil áderat adiuménti ad pulcritúdinem: 105
Capíllus passus, núdus pes, ipsa hórrida,
Lacrumaé, uestitus túrpis; ut, ni uís boni
In ípsa inesset fórma, haec formam exstínguerent.
Ille, qui íllam amabat fídicinam, tantúmmodo
'Satis' ínquit 'scitast'; nóster uero...

DA. Iám scio: 110
Amáre coepit.

GE. Scín quam? Quo euadát uide.
Postrídie ad anum récta pergit; óbsecrat,
Vt síbi eius faciat cópiam. Illa enim sé negat
Neque eum aéquom aït facere: íllam ciuem esse Átticam,
Bonám bonis prognátam; si uxorém uelit, 115
Lege íd licere fácere; sin alitér, negat.
Nostér quid ageret néscire: et illam dúcere
Cupiébat et metuébat absentém patrem.

DA. Non, sí redisset, éi pater ueniám daret?

GE. Ille índotatam uírginem atque ignóbilem 120
Daret ílli? Numquam fáceret.

DA. Quid fit dénique?

GE. Quid fíat? Est parasítus quidam Phórmio,
Homó confidens: qui íllum di omnes pérduint!

DA. Quid is fécit?

GE. Hoc consílium, quod dicám, dedit:
'Lex ést, ut orbae, quí sint genere próxumi, 125
Eis núbant, et illos dúcere eadem haec léx iubet.

Ego té cognatum dícam et tibi scribám dicam;
Patérnum amicum me ádsimulabo uírginis;
Ad iúdices ueniémus: qui fuerít pater,
Quae máter, qui cognáta tibi sit, ómnia haec 130
Confíngam: quod erit míhi bonum atque cómmodum,
Quom tu hórum nihil refélles, uincam scílicet.
Pater áderit; mihi parátae lites: quíd mea?
Illá quidem nostra erít.'

DA. Iocularem audáciam!

GE. Persuásumst homini: fáctumst; uentumst; uíncimur;
Duxít.

DA. Quid narras?

GE. Hóc, quod audis.

DA. Ó Geta, 136
Quid té futurumst?

GE. Néscio hercle; unum hóc scio:
Quod fórs feret, ferémus aequo animó.

DA. Placet.
Hem, istúc uirist offícium.

GE. In me omnis spés mihist.

DA. Laudo.

GE. Ád precatorem ádeam credo, quí mihi 140
Sic óret: 'Nunc amítte, quaeso, hunc; céterum
Posthác si quicquam, níl precor.' Tantúmmodo
Non áddit: 'Vbi ego hinc ábiero, uel occídito.'

DA. Quid paédagogus ílle, qui citharístriam?
Quid réi gerit?

GE. Sic, ténuiter.

DA. Non múltum habet, 145
Quod dét, fortasse?

GE. Ímmo nil nisi spém meram.

DA. Pater éius rediit án non?

GE. Nondum.
DA. Quíd? senem
Quoad éxspectatis uéstrum?
GE. Non certúm scio,
Sed epístulam ab eo adlátam esse audiuí modo
Et ad pórtitores ésse delatam: hánc petam. 150
DA. Num quíd, Geta, aliud mé uis?
GE. Vt bene sít tibi.
Puer, héus.—Nemon hoc pródit?—Cape, da hoc Dórcio.

ACTVS II

ANTIPHO PHAEDRIA

Advlescentes II

AN. Ádeon rem redísse, ut qui mi cónsultum optumé uelit esse,
Phaédria, patrem ut éxtimescam, ubi ín mentem eius aduénti ueniat!
Quód ni fuissem incógitans, ita éxspectarem, ut pár fuit.
PH. Quid istúc?
AN. Rogitas? quí tam audacis fácinoris mihi cónsciu's?
Quód utinam ne Phórmioni id suádere in mentem íncidisset 157
Neú me cupidum eo ínpulisset, quód mihi principiúmst mali!
Nón potitus éssem: fuisset tum íllos mi aegre aliquót dies,
At nón cottidiána cura haec ángeret animum,
PH. Aúdio.
AN. Dum exspécto, quam mox uéniat, qui adimat hánc mihi consuetúdinem. 161
PH. Aliís quia defit, quód amant, aegrest; tíbi quia superést dolet:
Amóre abundas, Ántipho.
Nam túa quidem hercle cérto uita haec éxpetenda optándaque est.
Ita mé di bene ament, út mihi liceat tám diu quod amó frui, 165

Iam dépecisci mórte cupio: tú conicito cétera,
Quid ego éx hac inopiá nunc capiam et quíd tu ex istac cópia;
Vt ne áddam, quod sine súmptu ingenuam, líberalem náctus es,
Quod habés, ita ut uoluísti, uxorem síne mala famá palam:
Beátus, ni unum désit, animus, quí modeste istaéc ferat.
Quod sí tibi res sit cum éo lenone, quó mihist, tum séntias. 171
Ita plérique ingenió sumus omnes: nóstri nosmet paénitet.

AN. At tú mihi contra núnc uidere fórtunatus, Phaédria,
Quoi de íntegro est potéstas etiam cónsulendi, quíd uelis:
Retinére amorem an míttere; ego in eum íncidi infelíx locum, 175
Vt néque mihi eius sit ámittendi néc retinendi cópia.
Sed quíd hoc est? Videon égo Getam curréntem huc aduenire?
Is est ípsus. Ei, timeó miser, quam hic míhi nunc nuntiét rem.

GETA ANTIPHO PHAEDRIA
Servos *Advlescentes II*

GE. Núllu's, Getá, nisi aliquod iam consilium célere reperies:
Íta nunc inparátum subito tánta te inpendént mala;
Quae néque uti deuitém scio neque quó modo me inde éxtraham: 181
Nam nón potest celári nostra díutius iam audácia.

AN. Quid íllic commotús uenit?

Ge. Tum témporis mihi púnctum ad hanc rem est: érus adest.
An. Quid illúc malist?
Ge. Quód quom audierit, quód eius remedium ínueniam iracúndiae? 185
Loquárne? incendam; táceam? instigem; púrgem me? laterém lauem.
Heú me miserum! Quóm mihi paueo, tum Ántipho me excrúciat animi:
Eíus me miseret, éi nunc timeo, is núnc me retinet; nam ábsque eo esset,
Récte ego mihi uidíssem et senis essem últus iracúndiam:
Áliquid conuasássem atque hinc me cónicerem protinam ín pedes. 190
An. Quamnam híc fugam aut furtúm parat?
Ge. Sed ubi Ántiphonem réperiam? aut qua quaérere insistám uia?
Ph. Te nóminat.
An. Nescío quod magnum hoc núntio exspectó malum.
Ph. Ah, sánun es?
Ge. Domum íre pergam; ibi plúrimumst.
Ph. Reuocémus hominem.
An. Sta ílico.
Ge. Hem, sátĭs pro imperio, quísquis es. 195
An. Geta.
Ge. Ípsest, quem uolui óbuiam.
An. Cédo, quid portas, óbsecro? atque id, sí potes, uerbo éxpedi.
Ge. Fáciam.
An. Eloquere.
Ge. Módo apud portum...

AN. Méumne?
GE. Intellexti.
AN. Óccidi.
PH. Hem.
AN. Quíd agam?
PH. Quid aïs?
GE. Huíus patrem uidísse me, patruóm tuom.
AN. Námquod ego huic nunc súbito exitio rémedium inueniám miser? 200
Quód si eo meae fortúnae redeunt, Phánium, abs te ut dístrahar,
Núllast mihi uita éxpetenda.
GE. Ergo, ístaec quom ita sint, Ántipho,
Tánto magis te aduígilare aequomst: fórtis fortuna ádiuuat.
AN. Nón sum apud me.
GE. Atqui ópus est, nunc quom máxume ut sis, Ántipho;
Nám si senserít te timidum páter esse, arbitrábitur 205
Cómmeruisse cúlpam.
PH. Hoc uerumst.
AN. Nón possum immutárier.
GE. Quíd faceres, si aliúd quid grauius tíbi nunc faciundúm foret?
AN. Quom hóc non possum, illúd minus possem.
GE. Hoc níhil est, Phaedria; ílicet.
Quíd hic conterimus óperam frustra? Quín abeo?
PH. Et quidem ego?
AN. Óbsecro,
Quíd si adsimulo? Sátinest?
GE. Garris.
AN. Vóltum contemplámini: me, 210
Sátine sic est?

GE. Nón.
AN. Quid si sic?
GE. Própemodum.
AN. Quid síc?
GE. Sat est:
Hem, istuc serua; et uérbum uerbo pár pari ut respóndeas,
Né te iratus súis saeuidicis díctis protelét.
AN. Scio.
GE. Ví coactum te ésse inuitum.
PH. Lége, iudició.
GE. Tenes?
Séd hic quis est senéx, quem uideo in última platea? Ípsus est. 215
AN. Non póssum adesse.
GE. Ah, quíd agis? quo abis, Ántipho?
Mane, ínquam.
AN. Egomet me nóui et peccatúm meum:
Vobís commendo Phánium et uitám meam.—
PH. Geta, quíd nunc fiet?
GE. Tú iam litis aúdies;
Ego pléctar pendens, nísi quid me feféllerit. 220
Sed quód modo hic nos Ántiphonem mónuimus,
Id nósmet ipsos fácere oportet, Phaédria.
PH. Aufér mi 'oportet': quín tu quid faciam ímpera.
GE. Meminístin, olim ut fúerit uostra orátio
In re íncipiunda ad défendendam nóxiam 225
Iustam íllam causam, fácilem, uincibilem, óptumam?
PH. Memini.
GE. Hem nunc ipsast ópus ea aut, si quíd potest,
Melióre et callidióre.
PH. Fiet sédulo.

GE. Nunc príor adito tu, égo in insidiis híc ero
Subcénturiatus, sí quid deficiás.
PH. Age. 230

DEMIPHO PHAEDRIA GETA
Senex *Advlescens* *Servos*

DE. Ítane tandem uxórem duxit Ántipho iniussú meo?
Néc meum imperium—ac mítto imperium—nón simultatém meam
Reueréri saltem! Nón pudere! O fácinus audax, ó Geta
Monitór!
GE. Vix tandem!
DE. Quíd mihi dicent aút quam causam réperient?
Demíror.
GE. Atqui réperiam: aliud cúra.
DE. An hoc dicét mihi: 235
'Inuítus feci; léx coégit'? Aúdio, fateór.
GE. Places.
DE. Verúm scientem, tácitum causam trádere aduersáriis,
Etiámne id lex coegit?
PH. Illud dúrum.
GE. Ego expediám: sine.
DE. Incértumst quid agam, quía praeter spem atque íncredibile hoc mi óptigit:
Ita sum ínritatus, ánimum ut nequeam ad cógitandum instítuere. 240
Quam ob rem ómnis, quom secúndae res sunt máxume, tum máxume
Meditári secum opórtet, quo pacto áduorsam aerumnám ferant;
Perícla, damna, exsília peregre rédiens semper cógitet,

Aut fíli peccatum aút uxoris mórtem aut morbum filiae;
Commúnia esse haec, fíeri posse, ut né quid animo sít nouom; 245
Quidquíd praeter spem euéniat, omne id députare esse ín lucro.

GE. O Phaédria, incredíbilest quantum erum ánte eo sapiéntia.
Meditáta mihi sunt ómnia mea incómmoda, erus si rédierit:
Moléndum usque in pistríno, uapulándum, habendae cómpedes,
Opus rúri faciundum: hórum nil quicquam áccidet animó nouom. 250
Quidquíd praeter spem euéniet, omne id députabo esse ín lucro.
Séd quid cessas hóminem adire et blánde in principio ádloqui?

DE. Phaédriam mei frátris uideo fílium mi ire óbuiam.

PH. Mi pátrue, salue.

DE. Sálue; sed ubist Antipho?

PH. Saluóm uenire...

DE. Crédo; hoc respondé mihi. 255

PH. Valet, híc est; sed satine ómnia ex senténtia?

DE. Vellém quidem.

PH. Quid istúc est?

DE. Rogitas, Phaédria?
Bonás me absente hic cónfecistis núptias.

PH. Eho, an íd suscenses núnc illi?

GE. Artificém probum!

DE. Egon ílli non suscénseam? Ipsum géstio 260
Dari mi ín conspectum, núnc sua culpa út sciat
Leném patrem illum fáctum me esse acérrimum.

PH. Atquí nil fecit, pátrue, quod suscénseas.
DE. Ecce aútem similia ómnia! Omnes cóngruont:
Vnúm quom noris, ómnis noris.
PH. Haúd itast. 265
DE. Hic in nóxiast, ille ád dicendam caúsam adest;
Quom illést, hic praestost: trádunt operas mútuas.
GE. Probe hórum facta inprúdens depinxít senex.
DE. Nam ni haéc ita essent, cum íllo haud stares, Phaédria.
PH. Si est, pátrue, culpam ut Ántipho in se admíserit, 270
Ex quá re minus rei fóret aut famae témperans,
Non caúsam dico, quín quod meritus sít ferat.
Sed sí quis forte málitia fretús sua
Insídias nostrae fécit adulescéntiae
Ac uícit, nostran cúlpa east an iúdicum, 275
Qui saépe propter ínuidiam adimunt díuiti
Aut própter misericórdiam addunt paúperi?
GE. Ni nóssem causam, créderem uera húnc loqui.
DE. An quísquam iudex ést, qui possit nóscere
Tua iústa, ubi tute uérbum non respóndeas, 280
Ita ut ílle fecit?
PH. Fúnctus adulescéntulist
Offícium liberális: postquam ad iúdices
Ventúmst, non potuit cógitata próloqui;
Ita éum tum timidum illíc obstupefecít pudor.
GE. Laudo húnc. Sed cesso adíre quam primúm senem?
Ere, sálue; saluom te áduenisse gaúdeo.
DE. Oh, 286
Bone cústos, salue, cólumen uero fámiliae,
Quoi cómmendaui fílium hinc abiéns meum!
GE. Iam dúdum te omnis nós accusare aúdio
Inmérito et me horunc ómnium inmeritíssumo. 290
Namquíd me in hac re fácere uoluistí tibi?

Seruom hóminem causam oráre leges nón sinunt,
Neque téstimoni díctiost.

DE. Mitto ómnia:
Do istúc 'inprudens tímuit adulescéns,' sino
'Tu séruo's'; uerum sí cognatast máxume, 295
Non fuít necesse habére; sed id quod léx iubet,
Dotém daretis, quaéreret aliúm uirum.
Qua rátione inopem pótius ducebát domum?

GE. Non rátio, uerum argéntum deerat.

DE. Súmeret
Alicúnde.

GE. Alicunde? Níhil est dictu fácilius. 300

DE. Postrémo si nullo álio pacto, faénore.

GE. Hui, díxti pulcre! Síquidem quisquam créderet
Te uíuo.

DE. Non, non síc futurumst; nón potest.
Egon íllam cum illo ut pátiar nuptam unúm diem?
Nihil suáue meritumst. Hóminem conmonstrárier
Mihi istúm uolo aut ubi hábitet demonstrárier. 306

GE. Nempe Phórmionem?

DE. Istúm patronum múlieris.

GE. Iam fáxo hic aderit.

DE. Ántipho ubi nunc ést?

GE. Foris.

DE. Abi, Phaédria, eum requíre atque huc addúce.

PH. Eo:
Rectá uia quidem ílluc.

GE. Nempe ad Pámphilam. 310

DE. Ego déos penates hínc salutatúm domum
Deuértar; inde ibo ád forum atque aliquót mihi
Amícos aduocábo, ad hanc rem qui ádsient,
Vt ne ínparatus sím, si ueniat Phórmio.

ACTVS III

PHORMIO GETA

Parasitvs Servos

PH. Ítane patris aïs aduentum uéritum hinc abiisse?
GE. Ádmodum. 315
PH. Phánium relíctam solam?
GE. Síc.
PH. Et iratúm senem?
GE. Óppido.
PH. Ad te súmma solum, Phórmio, rerúm redit.
Túte hoc intristí; tibi omnest éxedendum: accíngere.
GE. Óbsecro te.
PH. Sí rogabit...
GE. Ín te spes est.
PH. Éccere,
Quíd si reddet?
GE. Tu ínpulisti.
PH. Síc, opinor.
GE. Súbueni. 320
PH. Cédo senem: iam instrúcta sunt mi in córde consilia ómnia.
GE. Quíd ages?
PH. Quid uis, nísi uti maneat Phánium atque ex crímine hoc
Ántiphonem erípiam atque in me omnem íram deriuém senis?

GE. Ó uir fortis átque amicu's. Vérum hoc saepe, Phórmio,
Véreor, ne istaec fórtitudo in néruom erumpat dénique.

PH. Ah, 325
Nón itast: factúmst periclum, iám pedum uisást uia.
Quót me censes hómines iam deuérberasse usque ád necem, 327
Cédodum, enumquam iniúriarum audísti mi scriptám dicam? 329

GE. Quí istuc?

PH. Quia non réte accipitri ténnitur neque míluo, 330
Quí male faciunt nóbis; illis, quí nil faciunt, ténnitur,
Quía enim in illis frúctus est, in íllis opera lúditur.
Áliis aliunde ést periclum, unde áliquid abradí potest:
Míhi sciunt nihil ésse. Dices 'dúcent damnatúm domum':
Álere nolunt hóminem edacem, et sápiunt mea senténtia, 335
Pró maleficio sí beneficium súmmum nolunt réddere.

GE. Nón potest satis pro mérito ab illo tíbi referri grátia.

PH. Immo enim nemo sátis pro merito grátiam regí refert.
Téne asymbolúm uenire unctum átque lautum e bálneis,
Ótiosum ab ánimo, quom ille et cúra et sumptu absúmitur! 340
Dúm tibi fit quod pláceat, ille ríngitur: tu rídeas,
Príor bibas, priór decumbas; céna dubia appónitur...

GE. Quíd istuc uerbi est?

PH. Vbi tu dubites, quíd sumas potíssumum.
Haéc, quom rationem íneas, quam sint suáuia et quam cára sint,

Éa qui praebet, nón tu hunc habeas pláne praesentém deum? 345

GE. Sénex adest: uide, quíd agas; prima cóitiost acérrima.
Si éam sustinuerís, postilla iam, út lubet, ludás licet.

DEMIPHO HEGIO CRATINVS CRITO PHORMIO GETA
Senex *Advocati III* *Parasitvs* *Servos*

DE. Enúmquam quoiquam cóntumeliósius
Audístis factam iniúriam quam haec ést mihi?
Adéste quaeso.

GE. Irátus est.

PH. Quin tu hóc age: 350
Iam ego húnc agitabo.—Pró deum immortálium,
Negat Phánium esse hanc síbi cognatam Démipho?
Hanc Démipho negat ésse cognatám?

GE. Negat.

PH. Neque eíus patrem se scíre qui fuerít?

GE. Negat.

DE. Ipsum ésse opinor, dé quo agebam: séquimini! 355

PH. Quia egéns relictast mísera, ignoratúr parens, 357
Neclégitur ipsa. Víde auaritia quíd facit.

GE. Si erum ínsimulabis málitiae, male aúdies.

DE. O audáciam! Etiam me últro accusatum áduenit.

PH. Nam iam ádulescenti níhil est quod suscénseam, 361
Si illúm minus norat: quíppe homo iam grándior,
Paupér, quoi in opere uíta erat, rurí fere
Se cóntinebat; íbi agrum de nostró patre
Coléndum habebat. Saépe interea míhi senex 365
Narrábat se hunc neclégere cognatúm suom;
At quém uirum! Quem ego uíderim in uita óptumum.

GE. Videás te atque illum nárras!

PH. In malám crucem!
Nam ni éum esse existumássem, numquam tám grauis
Ob hanc ínimicitias cáperem in uostram fámiliam, 370
Quam is áspernatur núnc tam inliberáliter.
GE. Pergín ero absenti mále loqui, inpuríssume?
PH. Dignum aútem hoc illost.
GE. Aín tandem, carcér?
DE. Geta!
GE. Bonórum extortor, légum contortór.
DE. Geta!
PH. Respónde.
GE. Quis homost? Éhem...
DE. Tace.
GE. Absentí tibi
Te indígnas seque dígnas contumélias 376
Numquám cessauit dícere hodie.
DE. Désine.
Aduléscens, primum abs te hóc bona ueniá peto,
Si tíbi placere pótis est, mi ut respóndeas:
Quem amícum tuom aïs fuísse istum, explaná mihi,
Et quí cognatum mé sibi esse díceret. 381
PH. Proinde éxpiscare, quási non nosses.
DE. Nóssem?
PH. Ita.
DE. Ego mé nego; tu quí aïs, redige in mémoriam.
PH. Eho tú, sobrinum túom non noras?
DE. Énicas.
Dic nómen.
PH. Nomen? Máxume.
DE. Quid núnc taces? 385
PH. Perii hércle, nomen pérdidi.
DE. Quid aïs?

PH. Geta,
Si méministi id, quod ólim dictumst, súbice. Hem,
Non díco: quasi non nósses, temptatum áduenis.
DE. Ego aútem tempto?
GE. Stílpo.
PH. Atque adeo quíd mea?
Stilpóst.
DE. Quem dixti?
PH. Stílponem inquam nóueras. 390
DE. Neque égo illum noram néc mihi cognatús fuit
Quisquam ístoc nomine.
PH. Ítane? Non te horúm pudet?
At sí talentum rém reliquissét decem,
DE. Di tíbi malefaciant!
PH. prímus esses mémoriter 394
Progéniem uostram usque áb auo atque atauo próferens.
DE. Ita ut dícis! Ego tum, quom áduenissem, quí mihi
Cognáta ea esset, dícerem: itidem tú face.
Cedo qui ést cognata?
GE. Eu, nóster, recte: heus tú, caue.
PH. Dilúcide expedíui quibus me opórtuit
Iudícibus; tum id si fálsum fuerat, fílius 400
Quor nón refellit?
DE. Fílium narrás mihi?
Quoius dé stultitia díci ut dignumst nón potest.
PH. At tú, qui sapiens és, magistratús adi,
Iudícium de eadem caúsa iterum ut reddánt tibi;
Quandóquidem solus régnas et solí licet 405
Hic de eádem causa bís iudicium apíscier.
DE. Etsí mihi facta iniúriast, uerúm tamen
Potiús quam litis sécter aut quam te aúdiam,
Itidem út cognata sí sit, id quod léx iubet

Dotís dare, abduce hánc, minas quinque áccipe. 410

PH. Hahahaé, homo suauis.

DE. Quíd est? Num iniquom póstulo?

An ne hóc quidem ego adipíscar, quod ius públicumst?

PH. Itan tándem, quaeso, item út meretricem ubi abúsus sis,

Mercédem dare lex iúbet eï atque amíttere?

An, ut né quid turpe cíuis in se admítteret 415

Proptér egestatem, próxumo iussást dari,

Vt cum úno aetatem dégeret? Quod tú uetas.

DE. Ita, próxumo quidem; át nos unde? aut quam ób rem?

PH. Ohe,

'Actum' áiunt 'ne agas.'

DE. Nón agam? Immo haud désinam,

Donéc perfecero hóc.

PH. Ineptis.

DE. Síne modo. 420

PH. Postrémo tecum níl rei nobis, Démipho, est;

Tuos ést damnatus gnátus, non tu; nám tua

Praetérierat iam ad dúcendum aetas.

DE. Ómnia haec

Illúm putato, quae égo nunc dico, dícere;

Aut quídem cum uxore hac ípsum prohibebó domo.

GE. Irátus est.

PH. Tuté idem melius féceris. 426

DE. Itane és paratus fácere me aduorsum ómnia,

Infélix?

PH. Metuit híc nos, tametsi sédulo

Dissímulat.

GE. Bene habent tíbi principia.

PH. Quín quod est

Ferúndum fers? Tuis dígnum factis féceris, 430

Vt amíci inter nos símus.

De. Egon tuam éxpetam
Amícitiam? aut te uísum aut auditúm uelim?

Ph. Si concordabis cum ílla, habebis quaé tuam
Senectútem oblectet: réspice aetatém tuam.

De. Te obléctet, tibi habe.

Ph. Mínue uero iram.

De. Hóc age; 435
Satis iám uerborumst: nísi tu properas múlierem
Abdúcere, ego illam eíciam. Dixi, Phórmio.

Ph. Si tu íllam attigeris sécus quam dignumst líberam,
Dicám tibi inpingam grándem. Dixi, Démipho.
Si quíd opus fuerit, heús, domo me!

Ge. Intéllego. 440

DEMIPHO GETA CRATINVS HEGIO CRITO
Senex Servos Advocati III

De. Quantá me cura et sóllicitudine ádficit
Gnatús, qui me et se hisce ínpediuit núptiis!
Neque mi ín conspectum pródit, ut saltém sciam,
Quid de éa re dicat quídue sit senténtiae.
Abi, uíse redierítne iam an nondúm domum. 445

Ge. Eó.—

De. Videtis, quo ín loco res haéc siet.
Quid agó? dic, Hegio.

He. Égo? Cratinum cénseo,
Si tíbi uidetur.

De. Díc, Cratine.

Cra. Méne uis?

De. Te.

Cra. Ego, quae ín rem tuam sint, éa uelim facías. Mihi

Sic hóc uidetur: quód te absente hic fílius 450
Egít, restitui in íntegrum aequomst ét bonum,
Et id ímpetrabis. Díxi.

DE. Dic nunc, Hégio.

HE. Ego sédulo hunc dixísse credo; uérum itast:
Quot hómines, tot senténtiae; suos quoíque mos.
Mihi nón uidetur, quód sit factum légibus, 455
Rescíndi posse; et túrpe inceptust.

DE. Díc, Crito.

CRI. Ego ámplius delíberandum cénseo:
Res mágnast.

CRA. Num quid nós uis?

DE. Fecistís probe:
Incértior sum múlto quam dudúm.—

GE. Negant
Redísse.

DE. Frater ést exspectandús mihi: 460
Is quód mihi dederit de hác re consilium, íd sequar.
Percóntatum ibo ad pórtum, quoad se récipiat.

GE. At ego Ántiphonem quaéram, ut quae acta hic sínt sciat.
Sed eccum ípsum uideo in témpore huc se récipere.

ANTIPHO GETA

Advlescens *Servos*

AN. Énimuero, Antiphó, multimodis cum ístoc animo es uítuperandus: 465
Ítane te hinc abísse et uitam tuám tutandam aliís dedisse!
Álios tuam rem crédidisti mágis quam tete animáduersuros?

Nam, útut erant alia, ílli certe, quaé nunc tibi domíst, consuleres,
Né quid propter túam fidem decépta poteretúr mali;
Quoí nunc miserae spés opesque súnt in te uno omnés sitae. 470

GE. Et quídem, ere, nos iam dúdum hic te absentem íncusamus, qui ábieris.
AN. Te ipsúm quaerebam.
GE. Séd ea causa níhilo magis defécimus.
AN. Loquere óbsecro, quonam ín loco sunt rés et fortunaé meae:
Num quíd patri subolét?
GE. Nil etiam.
AN. Ecquíd spei porrost?
GE. Néscio.
AN. Ah.
GE. Nisi Phaédria haud cessáuit pro te eníti.
AN. Nihil fecít noui. 475
GE. Tum Phórmio itidem in hác re ut aliis strénuom hominem praébuit.
AN. Quid is fécit?
GE. Confutáuit uerbis ádmodum iratúm senem.
AN. Eu, Phórmio.
GE. Ego, quod pótui, porro.
AN. Mí Geta, omnis uós amo.
GE. Síc habent princípia sese, ut díxi: adhuc tranquílla res est,
Mánsurusque pátruom pater est, dum húc adueniat.
AN. Quíd eum?
GE. Vt aibat 480
De eíus consilio sése uelle fácere, quód ad hanc rem áttinet.

AN. Quántum metuist míhi, uidere huc sáluom nunc patruóm, Geta!
Nam pér eius unam, ut aúdio, aut uiuam aút moriar senténtiam.

GE. Phaédria tibi adést.

AN. Vbinam?

GE. Eccum ab súa palaestra exít foras.

PHAEDRIA *Advlescens* DORIO *Leno* ANTIPHO *Advlescens* GETA *Servos*

PH. Dório, 485
Audi óbsecro.

DO. Non aúdio.

PH. Parúmper.

DO. Quin omítte me.

PH. Aúdi, quod dicam.

DO. Át enim taedet iam aúdire eadem míliens.

PH. Át nunc dicam, quód lubenter aúdias.

DO. Loquere, aúdio.

PH. Nón queo te exoráre, ut maneas tríduom hoc? Quo núnc abis?

DO. Mirábar, si tu míhi quicquam adferrés noui.

AN. Eí, 490
Metuo lenónem, ne quid...

GE. súo suat capiti? Ídem ego uereor.

PH. Nón mihi credis?

DO. Háriolare.

PH. Sín fidem do?

DO. Fábulae.

PH. Faéneratum istúc beneficium púlcre tibi dicés.

DO. Logi.

PH. Créde mihi, gaudébis facto; uérum hercle hoc est.
DO. Sómnia.
PH. Éxperire; nón est longum.
DO. Cántilenam eandém canis. 495
PH. Tu míhi cognatus, tú parens, tu amícus, tu...
DO. Garrí modo.
PH. Ádeon ingenio ésse duro te átque inexorábili,
V́t neque misericórdia neque précibus mollirí queas!
DO. Ádeon te esse incógitantem atque ínpudentem, Phaédria,
V́t phaleratis dúcas dictis me ét meam ductes grátiis!
AN. Míseritumst.
PH. Ei, uéris uincor!
GE. Quám uterquest similís sui!
PH. Atque Ántipho alia quom óccupatus ésset sollicitúdine, 502
Tum hoc ésse mi obiectúm malum!
AN. Ah, quid istúc est autem, Phaédria?
PH. Ó fortunatíssume Antipho!
AN. Égone?
PH. Quoi quod amás domist,
Néque cum huius modi umquam úsus uenit út conflictarés malo. 505
AN. Míhin domist? Immo, íd quod aiunt, aúribus teneó lupum.
Nám neque quo pacto á me amittam néque uti retineám scio.
DO. Ípsum istuc mihi in hóc est.
AN. Heia, né parum lenó sies.
Núm quid hic confécit?
PH. Hicine? quód homo inhumaníssumus:
Pámphilam meam uéndidit.

AN. Quid? uéndidit?
GE. Ain? uéndidit? 510
PH. Véndidit.
DO. Quam indígnum facinus, áncillam aere emptám meo!
PH. Néqueo exorare, út me maneat ét cum illo ut mutét fidem
Tríduom hoc, dum id quód est promissum ab amícis argentum aúfero.
Sí non tum dedero, únam praeterea hóram ne oppertús sies.
DO. Óptundes?
AN. Haud lóngumst id quod órat: exorét sine. 515
Ídem hic tibi, quod bóni promeritus fúeris, conduplicáuerit.
DO. Vérba istaec sunt.
AN. Pámphilamne hac úrbe priuarí sines?
Túm praeterea horúnc amorem dístrahi poterín pati?
DO. Néque ego neque tu...
PH. Dí tibi omnes íd, quod es dignús, duint!
DO. Égo te complurís aduorsum ingénium meum mensés tuli 520
Póllicitantem et níhil ferentem, fléntem; nunc contra ómnia haec
Répperi, qui dét neque lacrumet: dá locum melióribus.
AN. Cérte hercle, ego si sátis commemini, tíbi quidem est olím dies,
Quam ád dares huic, praéstituta.
PH. Fáctum.
DO. Num ego istúc nego?
AN. Iam éa praeteriit?
DO. Nón, uerum haec eï ántecessit.
AN. Nón pudet 525

Vánitatis?

DO. Mínime, dum ob rem.

GE. Stérculinum!

PH. Dório,

Ítane tandem fácere oportet?

DO. Síc sum: si placeo, útere.

AN. Síc hunc decipís!

DO. Immo enimuero, Ántipho, hic me décipit:
Nam híc me huius modi scíbat esse, ego húnc esse aliter crédidi;
Íste me feféllit; ego isti níhilo sum aliter ác fui. 530
Séd utut haec sunt, támen hoc faciam: crás mane argentúm mihi
Míles dare se díxit; si mihi príor tu attuleris, Phaédria,
Meá lege utar, út potior sit, quí prior ad dandúmst. Vale!

PHAEDRIA ANTIPHO GETA
Advlescentes II *Servos*

PH. Quíd faciam? Vnde ego núnc tam subito huic árgentum inueniám miser,
Quoí minus nihilost? Quód, hic si pote fuísset exorárier
Tríduom hoc, promíssum fuerat.

AN. Ítane hunc patiemúr, Geta, 536
Fíeri miserum, quí me dudum, ut díxti, adiuerit cómiter?
Quín, quom opust, benefícium rursum eï éxperiemur réddere?

GE. Scío equidem hoc esse aéquom.

AN. Age ergo, sólus seruare húnc potes.

GE. Quíd faciam?
AN. Inueniás argentum.
GE. Cúpio; sed id unde, édoce. 540
AN. Páter adest hic.
GE. Scío; sed quid tum?
AN. Ah, díctum sapientí sat est.
GE. Ítane?
AN. Ita.
GE. Sane hércle pulcre suádes: etiam tu hínc abis?
Nón triumpho, ex núptiis tuis sí nihil nanciscór mali,
Ni étiam nunc me huius caúsa quaerere ín malo iubeás crucem?
AN. Vérum hic dicit.
PH. Quíd? ego uobis, Géta, alienus sum?
GE. Haúd puto; 545
Séd parumne est quod ómnibus nunc nóbis suscensét senex,
Ni ínstigemus étiam, ut nullus lócus relinquatúr preci?
PH. Álius ab oculís meis illam in ígnotum abducét locum? Hem:
Tum ígitur, dum licét dumque adsum, lóquimini mecum, Ántipho,
Cóntemplaminí me.
AN. Quam ob rem? aut quídnam facturú's? cedo. 550
PH. Quóquo hinc asportábitur terrárum, certumst pérsequi
Aút perire.
GE. Dí bene uortant quód agas! pedetemptím tamen.
AN. Víde, si quid opis pótes adferre huic.
GE. 'Sí quid'? quid?
AN. Quaere óbsecro:
Né quid plus minúsue faxit, quód nos post pigeát, Geta.

GE. Quaéro.—Saluos ést, ut opinor; uérum enim metuó malum. 555
AN. Nóli metuere: úna tecum bóna mala tolerábimus.
GE. Quántum opus est tibi argénti, loquere.
PH. Sólae trigintá minae.
GE. Tríginta? Hui, percárast, Phaedria.
PH. Ístaec uero uílis est.
GE. Áge age, inuentas réddam.
PH. O lepidum!
GE. Aufér te hinc!
PH. Iam opust.
GE. Iám feres:
Séd opus est mihi Phórmionem ad hánc rem adiutorém dari. 560
PH. Praéstost: audacíssume oneris quíduis inpone, híc feret;
Sólus est homo amíco amicus.
GE. Eámus ergo ad eum ócius!
AN. Núm quid ĕst, quod operá mea uobis ópŭs sit?
GE. Nihil; uerum ábi domum
Ét illam miseram, quam égo nunc intus scío esse exanimatám metu,
Cónsolare. Céssas?
AN. Nihil est, aéque quod faciám lubens. 565
PH. Quá uia istuc fácies?
GE. Dicam in itínere: modo te hinc ámoue!

ACTVS IV

DEMIPHO CHREMES

Senes II

DE. Quid? quá profectus caúsa hinc es Lemnúm, Chremes,
Addúxtin tecum fíliam?
CH. Non.
DE. Quíd ita non?
CH. Postquám uidet me eius máter esse hic diútius,
Simul aútem non manébat aetas uírginis 570
Meam néclegentiam, ípsam cum omni fámilia
Ad mé profectam esse aíbant.
DE. Quid illi tám diu
Quaeso ígitur commorábare, ubi id audíeras?
CH. Pol mé detinuit mórbus.
DE. Vnde? aut quí?
CH. Rogas?
Senéctus ipsast mórbus. Sed uenísse eas 575
Saluás audiui ex naúta, qui illas uéxerat.
DE. Quid gnáto optigerit me ábsente, audistí, Chremes?
CH. Quod quídem me factum cónsili incertúm facit.
Nam hanc cóndicionem sí quoi tulero extrário,
Quo pácto aut unde míhi sit, dicundum órdinest.
Te míhi fidelem esse aéque atque egomet súm mihi
Scibam. Ílle si me aliénus adfiném uolet, 582
Tacébit, dum intercédet familiáritas;

Sin spréuerit me, plús quam opus est scitó sciet.
Vereórque, ne uxor áliqua hoc resciscát mea. 585
Quod sí fit, ut me excútiam atque egrediár domo,
Id réstat; nam ego meórum solus súm meus.
DE. Scio ita ésse; et istaec míhi res sollicitúdinist,
Neque défetiscar úsque adeo experírier,
Donéc tibi id, quod póllicitus sum, effécero. 590

GETA DEMIPHO CHREMES
Servos *Senes II*

GE. Ego hóminem callidiórem uidi néminem
Quam Phórmionem. Vénio ad hominem, ut dícerem
Argéntum opus esse et íd quo pacto fíeret.
Vixdúm dimidium díxeram, intelléxerat:
Gaudébat, me laudábat, quaerebát senem. 595
Dis grátias agébat, tempus síbi dari,
Vbi Phaédriae esse osténderet nihiló minus
Amícum sese quam Ántiphoni. Hominem ád forum
Iussi ópperiri: eo me ésse adducturúm senem.
Sed eccum ípsum. Quis est ultérior? Attat, Phaédriae
Pater uénit. Sed quid pértimui autem bélua? 601
An quía quos fallam pro úno duo sunt míhi dati?
Commódius esse opínor duplici spe útier.
Petam hínc, unde a primo ínstiti: is si dát, sat est;
Si ab éo nil fiet, tum húnc adoriar hóspitem. 605

ANTIPHO GETA CHREMES DEMIPHO
Advlescens *Servos* *Senes II*

AN. Exspécto, quam mox récipiat sesé Geta.
Sed pátruom uideo cúm patre adstantem. Eí mihi,
Quam tímeo, aduentus húius quo inpellát patrem!

GE. Adíbo: o salue, nóster Chremes!

CH. Salué, Geta!

GE. Veníre saluom uólup est.

CH. Credo.

GE. Quíd agitur? 610

Multa áduenienti, ut fít, noua hic?

CH. Complúria.

GE. Ita. De Ántiphone audístin quae facta?

CH. Ómnia.

GE. Tun díxeras huic? Fácinus indignúm, Chremes,

Sic círcumiri!

CH. Id cum hóc agebam cómmodum.

GE. Nam hercle égo quoque id quidem ágitans mecum sédulo 615

Inuéni, opinor, rémedium huic rei.

CH. Quíd, Geta?

DE. Quod rémedium?

GE. Vt abii ábs te, fit forte óbuiam

Mihi Phórmio?

CH. Qui Phórmio?

DE. Is, qui istánc...

CH. Scio.

GE. Visúmst mihi, ut eius témptarem senténtiam.

Prendo hóminem solum: 'Quór non' inquam, 'Phórmio, 620

Vidés, inter nos síc haec potius cúm bona

Vt cómponamus grátia quam cúm mala?

Erus líberalis ést et fugitans lítium;

Nam céteri quidem hércle amici omnés modo

Vno óre auctores fuére, ut praecipitem hánc daret.'

AN. Quid hic coéptat aut quo euádet hodie?

GE. 'An légibus 626

Datúrum poenas díces, si illam eiécerit?
Iam id éxploratumst: heía, sudabís satis,
Si cum íllo inceptas hómine: ea eloquéntiast.
Verúm pono esse uíctum eum; at tandém tamen 630
Non cápitis ei res ágitur, sed pecúniae.'
Postquam hóminem his uerbis séntio mollírier,
'Solí sumus nunc hic' ínquam; 'eho dic, quid uís dari
Tibi ín manum, ut erus hís desistat lítibus,
Haec hínc facessat, tú molestus né sies?' 635

AN. Satin ílli di sunt própitii?

GE. 'Nam sát scio,
Si tu áliquam partem aequí bonique díxeris,
Vt est ílle bonus uir, tría non commutábitis
Verba hódie inter uos.'

DE. Quís te istaec iussít loqui?

CH. Immó non potuit mélius peruenírier 640
Eo, quó nos uolumus.

AN. Óccidi.

DE. Perge éloqui.

GE. A prímo homo insaníbat.

CH. Cedo, quid póstulat?

GE. Quid? nímium quantum.

CH. Quántum? dic.

GE. Si quís daret
Taléntum magnum.

DE. Immó malum hercle: ut níhil pudet!

GE. Quod díxi adeo eï: 'Quaéso, quid si fíliam 645
Suam únicam locáret? Parui rétulit
Non súscepisse: inuéntast, quae dotém petat.'
Vt ad paúca redeam ac míttam illius inéptias,
Haec dénique eius fúit postrema orátio:

'Ego' ínquit 'a princípio amici fíliam, 650
Ita ut aéquom fuerat, uólui uxorem dúcere;
Nam míhi uenibat ín mentem eius incómmodum,
In séruitutem paúperem ad ditém dari.
Sed mi ópus erat, ut apérte tibi nunc fábuler,
Aliquántulum quae adférret, qui dissóluerem 655
Quae débeo; et etiám nunc, si uolt Démipho
Dare quántum ab hac accípio, quae sponsást mihi,
Nullám mihi malim quam ístanc uxorém dari.'

AN. Vtrúm stultitia fácere ego hunc an málitia
Dicám, scientem an ínprudentem, incértus sum. 660

DE. Quid si ánimam debet?

GE. 'Áger oppositust pígnori
Ob décem minas est.'

DE. Áge age, iam ducát: dabo.

GE. 'Aedículae item sunt ób decem alias.'

DE. Oíeï,
Nimiúmst.

CH. Ne clama: répetito hasce a mé decem.

GE. 'Vxóri emunda ancíllulast; tum plúscula 665
Supelléctile opus est, ópus est sumptu ad núptias:
His rébus sane póne' inquit 'decém minas.'

DE. Sescéntas proinde scríbito iam míhi dicas:
Nihil do. Ínpuratus me ílle ut etiam inrídeat?

CH. Quaeso, égo dabo, quiésce: tu modo fílium 670
Fac ut íllam ducat, nós quam uolumus.

AN. Eí mihi!
Geta, óccidisti mé tuis falláciis.

CH. Mea caúsa eïcitur; mé hoc est aequom amíttere.

GE. 'Quantúm potest me cértiorem' inquít 'face,
Si illám dant, hanc ut míttam, ne incertús siem; 675
Nam illí mihi dotem iám constituerúnt dare.'

CH. Iam accípiat: illis répudium renúntiet;
Hanc dúcat.

DE. Quae quidem ílli res uortát male!

CH. Oppórtune adeo argéntum nunc mecum áttuli,
Fructúm, quem Lemni uxóris reddunt praédia. 680
Inde súmam; uxori tíbi opus esse díxero.

ANTIPHO GETA

Advlescens *Servos*

AN. Geta.

GE. Hém.

AN. Quid egisti?

GE. Émunxi argentó senes.

AN. Satine ést id?

GE. Nescio hércle: tantum iússus sum.

AN. Eho, uérbero, aliud míhi respondes ác rogo?

GE. Quid érgo narras?

AN. Quíd ego narrem? Operá tua 685
Ad réstim mihi quidém res redit planíssume.
Vt té quidem omnes dí deae superi ínferi
Malís exemplis pérdant! Hem, si quíd uelis,
Huic mándes, qui te ad scópulum e tranquillo aúferat.
Quid mínus utibile fúit quam hoc ulcus tángere 690
Aut nóminare uxórem? Iniectast spés patri
Posse íllam extrudi. Cédo nunc porro: Phórmio
Dotém si accipiet, úxor ducendást domum:
Quid fíet?

GE. Non enim dúcet.

AN. Noui. Céterum
Quom argéntum repetent, nóstra causa scílicet 695
In néruom potius íbit.

GE. Nihil est, Ántipho,

Quin mále narrando póssit deprauárier.
Tu id, quód bonist, excérpis, dicis quód malist.
Audí nunc contra: iám si argentum accéperit,
Ducéndast uxor, út aïs (concedó tibi): 700
Spatiúm quidem tandem ápparandi núptias,
Vocándi, sacruficándi dabitur paúlulum.
Intérea amici quód polliciti súnt dabunt:
Inde íste reddet.

AN. Quam ób rem? aut quid dicét?

GE. Rogas?
'Quot rés postilla mónstra euenerúnt mihi! 705
Intro íit in aedis áter alienús canis,
Anguís in inpluuium décidit de tégulis,
Gallína cecinit; ínterdixit háriolus,
Harúspex uetuit; ánte brumam autém noui
Negóti incipere...
...' quaé causast iustíssuma. 710
Haec fíent.

AN. Vt modo fíant!

GE. Fient: mé uide.
Pater éxit: abi, dic ésse argentum Phaédriae.

DEMIPHO CHREMES GETA

Senes II *Servos*

DE. Quiétus esto, inquam; égo curabo, né quid uerborúm duit.
Hoc témere numquam amíttam ego a me, quín mihi testis ádhibeam:
Quoi dem ét quam ob rem dem, cómmemorabo.

GE. Vt caútus est, ubi níl opust. 715

CH. Atque íta opus factost; ét matura, dúm lubido eadem haéc manet:

Nam si áltera illaec mágis instabit, fórsitan nos réiciat.

GE. Rem ipsám putasti.

DE. Dúc me ad eum ergo.

GE. Nón moror.

CH. Vbi hoc égeris,

Transíto ad uxorém meam, ut conuéniat hanc prius quam hínc abit.

Dicát eam dare nos Phórmioni núptum, ne suscénseat; 720

Et mágis esse illum idóneum, qui ipsí sit familiárior;

Nos nóstro officio nón digressos ésse: quantum is uóluerit,

Datum ésse dotis.

DE. Quíd tua malum id réfert?

CH. Magni, Démipho.

Non sátis est tuom te offícium fecisse, íd si non fama ádprobat:

Volo ípsius uoluntáte haec fieri, né se eiectam praédicet. 725

DE. Idem égo istuc facere póssum.

CH. Mulier múlieri magis cónuenit.

DE. Rogábo.

CH. Vbi illas núnc ego reperíre possim, cógito.

SOPHRONA CHREMES

Nvtrix *Senex*

So. Quíd agam? quem mi amícum inueniam mísera? aut quo consília haec referam?

Aút unde auxiliúm petam?

Nám uereor, era ne ób meum suasum indígna iniuria ádficiatur: 730

Íta patrem adulescéntis facta haec tólerare audió
uiolenter.

CH. Námquae haec anus est, éxanimata a frátre quae
egressást meo?

So. Quod ut fácerem egestas me ínpulit, quom scírem
infirmas núptias

Hasce ésse, ut id consúlerem, interea uíta ut in tutó
foret.

CH. Cérte edepol, nisi me ánimus fallit aút parum pro-
spíciunt oculi, 735

Meaé nutricem gnátae uideo.

So. Néque ille inuestigátur,

CH. Quid ago?

So. Qui ést eius pater.

CH. Ádeo, maneo, dum haéc quae loquitur
mágis cognosco?

So. Quód si eum nunc reperíre possim, níhil est, quod uereár.

CH. East ipsa:

Cónloquar.

So. Quis hic lóquitur?

CH. Sophrona.

So. Ét meum nomen nóminat?

CH. Réspice ad me.

So. Di óbsecro uos, éstne hic Stilpo?

CH. Nón.

So. Negas? 740

CH. Cóncede hinc a fóribus paulum istórsum sodes,
Sóphrona.

Ne me ístoc posthac nómine appellássis.

So. Quid? non óbsecro es,

Quem sémper te esse díctitasti?

CH. St'.

So. Quid has metuís foris?
Ch. Conclúsam hic habeo uxórem saeuam. Vérum istoc me nómine
Eo pérperam olim díxi, ne uos fórte inprudentés foris 745
Effútiretis átque id porro aliqua úxor mea rescísceret.
So. Istóc pol nos te hic ínuenire míserae numquam pótuimus.
Ch. Eho díc mihi, quid reí tibist cum fámilia hac, unde éxis? Vbi illaé sunt?
So. Miseram me!
Ch. Hém, quid est? uiuóntne?
So. Viuit gnáta.
Matrem ípsam ex aegritúdine hac miserám mors consecútast. 750
Ch. Male fáctum.
So. Ego autem, quae éssem anus desérta, egens, ignóta,
Vt pótui nuptum uírginem locáui huic adulescénti,
Harúm qui est dominus aédium.
Ch. Antiphónin?
So. Em istic ípsi.
Ch. Quid? duásne uxores hábet?
So. Au, obsecro, únam ille quidem hanc sólam.
Ch. Quid illam álteram, quae dícitur cognáta?
So. Haec ergost.
Ch. Quíd aïs? 755
So. Compósito factumst, quó modo hanc amáns habere pósset
Sine dóte.
Ch. Di uostrám fidem, quam saépe forte témere
Euéniunt, quae non aúdeas optáre! Offendi aduéniens,
Quocúm uolebam et út uolebam cónlocatam gnátam.

Quod nós ambo opere máxumo dabámus operam ut fíeret, 760
Sine nóstra cura, máxuma sua cúra haec sola fécit.

So. Nunc quíd opus facto sít uide: pater ádulescentis uénit
Eumque ánimo iniquo hoc óppido ferre áiunt.

Ch. Nihil períclist.
Sed pér deos atque hómines meam esse hanc cáue resciscat quísquam.

So. Nemo é me scibit.

Ch. Séquere me: intus cétera audietis. 765

ACTVS V

DEMIPHO GETA

Senex *Servos*

DE. Nostrápte culpa fácimus, ut malís expediat ésse,
Dum nímium dici nós bonos studémus et benígnos.
Ita fúgias, ne praetér casam, quod áiunt. Nonne id sát erat,
Accípere ab illo iniúriam? Etiam argéntumst ultro obiéctum,
Vt sít, qui uiuat, dum áliud aliquid flágiti confíciat. 770
GE. Planíssume.
DE. Eis nunc praémiumst, qui récta praua fáciunt...
GE. Veríssume.
DE. Vt stultíssume quidem illí rem gesserímus.
GE. Modo ut hóc consilio póssiet discédi, ut istam dúcat.
DE. Etiámne id dubiumst?
GE. Haúd scio hercle, ut homóst, an mutet ánimum.
DE. Hem, mútet autem?
GE. Néscio; uerúm, si forte, díco. 775
DE. Ita fáciam, ut frater cénsuit, ut uxórem eius huc addúcam,
Cum ista út loquatur. Tú, Geta, abi prae, núntia hanc uentúram.—
GE. Argéntum inuentumst Phaédriae; de iúrgio silétur;
Prouísumst, ne in praeséntia haec hinc ábeat: quid nunc pórro?

Quid fíet? In eodém luto haesitás: uorsura sólues, 780
Geta; praésens quod fuerát malum, in diem ábiit; plagae créscunt,
Nisi próspicis. Nunc hínc domum ibo ac Phánium edocébo,
Ne quíd uereatur Phórmionem aut huíus oratiónem.

DEMIPHO NAVSISTRATA
Senex *Mvlier*

DE. Agedum, út soles, Nausístrata, fac illa út placetur nóbis,
Vt súa uoluntate íd, quod est faciúndum, faciat.
NA. Fáciam. 785
DE. Paritér nunc opera me ádiuues, ac ré dudum opituláta's.
NA. Factúm uolo; ac pol mínus queo uiri cúlpa quam me dígnumst.
DE. Quid aútem?
NA. Quia pol meí patris bene párta indiligénter
Tutátur; nam ex eis praédiis talénta argenti bína
Statím capiebat. Vír uiro quid praéstat!
DE. Binan quaéso? 790
NA. Ac rébus uilióribus multó talenta bína.
DE. Hui.
NA. Quid haéc uidentur?
DE. Scílicet.
NA. Virúm me natum uéllem:
Ego osténderem,
DE. Certó scio.
NA. quo pácto...
DE. Parce sódes,
Vt póssis cum illa, né te adulescens múlier defetíget.
NA. Faciam, út iubes. Sed meúm uirum abs te exíre uideo.

NAVSISTRATA CHREMES DEMIPHO

Mvlier *Senes II*

CH. Ehem, Démipho. 795

Iam illí datumst argéntum?

DE. Curaui ílico.

CH. Nollém datum.

Ei, uídeo uxorem: paéne plus quam sát erat.

DE. Quor nollés, Chremes?

CH. Iam récte.

DE. Quid tu? ecquíd locutu's cum ístac, quam ob rem hanc dúcimus?

CH. Transégi.

DE. Quid aït tándem?

CH. Abduci nón potest.

DE. Qui nón potest?

CH. Quia utérque utrique est córdi.

DE. Quid istuc nóstra?

CH. Magni; praéterhac 800

Cognátam comperi ésse nobis.

DE. Quíd? deliras.

CH. Síc erit.

Non témere dico: rédii mecum in mémoriam.

DE. Satin sánus es?

NA. Au, óbsecro, uide ne ín cognatam pécces.

DE. Non est.

CH. Né nega:

Patris nómen aliud díctumst; hoc tu errásti.

DE. Non norát patrem?

CH. Norát.

DE. Quor aliud díxit?

CH. Numquamne hódie concedés mihi 805

Neque intélleges?
DE. Si tú nil narras?
CH. Pérdis.
NA. Miror, quíd hoc siet.
DE. Equidem hércle nesció.
CH. Vin scire? At íta me seruet Iúppiter,
Vt própior illi, quám ego sum ac tu, némost.
DE. Di uostrám fidem,
Eámus ad ipsam: una ómnis nos aut scíre aut nescire hóc uolo.
CH. Ah.
DE. Quid ést?
CH. Itan paruam míhi fidem esse apúd te!
DE. Vin me crédere? 810
Vin sátis quaesitum mi ístuc esse? Age, fíat. Quid? illa fília
Amíci nostri quíd futurumst?
CH. Récte.
DE. Hanc igitur míttimus?
CH. Quid ni?
DE. Ílla maneat?
CH. Síc.
DE. Ire igitur tíbi licet, Nausístrata.
NA. Sic pól commodius ésse in omnis árbitror, quam ut coéperas,
Manére hanc; nam perlíberalis uísast, quom uidí, mihi.— 815
DE. Quid istúc negotist?
CH. Iámne operuit óstium?
DE. Iam.
CH. O Iúppiter,
Di nós respiciunt: gnátam inueni núptam cum tuo fílio.

DE. Hem,

Quo pácto potuit?

CH. Nón satis tutus ést ad narrandum híc locus.

DE. At tu íntro abi!

CH. Heus, ne fílii quidem hoc nóstri resciscánt uolo.

ANTIPHO

Advlescens

Laetús sum, ut meae res sése habent, fratri óptigisse quód uolt. 820

Quam scítumst, eius modí parare in ánimo cupiditátes,

Quas, quóm res aduorsaé sient, pauló mederi póssis!

Hic símul argentum répperit, curá sese expedíuit;

Ego núllo possum rémedio me euóluere ex his túrbis,

Quin, si hóc celetur, ín metu, sin pátefit, in probró sim. 825

Neque mé domum nunc réciperem, ni mi ésset spes osténta

Huiúsce habendae. Séd ubinam Getam ínuenire póssim?

PHORMIO ANTIPHO

Parasitvs *Advlescens*

PH. Argéntum accepi, trádidi lenóni; abduxi múlierem,

Curáui, propria ut Phaédria poterétur; nam emissást manu. 830

Nunc úna mihi res étiam restat, quae ést conficiunda, ótium

Ab sénibus ad potándum ut habeam; nam áliquot hos sumám dies.

AN. Sed Phórmiost. Quid aís?

PH. Quid?

AN. Quidnam núnc facturust Phaédria?
Quo pácto satietátem amoris aít se uelle absúmere?
PH. Vicíssim partis túas acturus ést.
AN. Quas?
PH. Vt fugitét patrem. 835
Te súas rogauit rúrsum ut ageres, caúsam ut pro se díceres;
Nam pótaturus ést apud me. Ego me íre senibus Súnium
Dicam ád mercatum, ancíllulam emptum dúdum quam dixít Geta;
Ne quom híc non uideant mé conficere crédant argentúm suom.
Sed óstium concrépuit abs te.
AN. Víde quis egreditúr.
PH. Getast. 840

GETA ANTIPHO PHORMIO
Servos *Advlescens* *Parasitvs*

GE. Ó Fortuna, o Fórs Fortuna, quántis commoditátibus,
Quám subito meo ero Ántiphoni ope uóstra hunc onerastís diem!
AN. Quídnam hic sibi uolt?
GE. Nósque amicos eíus exonerastís metu!
Séd ego nunc mihi césso, qui non úmerum hunc onero pállio
Átque hominem propero ínuenire, ut haéc, quae contigerínt, sciat. 845
AN. Núm tu intellegís, quid hic narret?
PH. Núm tu?
AN. Nihil.
PH. Tantúndem ego.

GE. Ád lenonem hinc íre pergam; ibi núnc sunt.
AN. Heus, Geta!
GE. Hém tibi.
Núm mirum aut nouómst reuocari, cúrsum quom institerís?
AN. Geta!
GE. Pérgit hercle. Númquam tu odio túo me uinces.
AN. Nón manes?
GE. Vápula!
AN. Id quidem tíbi iam fiet, nísi resistis, uérbero. 850
GE. Fámiliariórem oportet ésse hunc: minitatúr malum.
Séd isne est, quem quaero, án non? Ipsust. Cóngredere actutúm.
AN. Quid est?
GE. O ómnium, quantúm est qui uiuont, hómo hominum ornatíssume!
Nám sine controuérsia ab dis sólus diligere, Ántipho.
AN. Íta uelim; sed quí istuc credam ita ésse, mihi dicí uelim. 855
GE. Sátine est, si te délibutum gaúdio reddo?
AN. Énicas.
PH. Quín tu hinc pollicitátiones aúfer et quod férs cedo.
GE. Oh,
Tú quoque aderas, Phórmio?
PH. Aderam; séd tu cessas?
GE. Áccipe, em:
Ýt modo argentúm tibi dedimus ápud forum, rectá domum
Súmus profecti; intérea mittit érus me ad uxorém tuam. 860
AN. Quam ób rem?
GE. Omitto próloqui: nam níhil ad hanc rem est, Ántipho.

Vbi in gynaeceum íre occipio, púer ad me accurrít Mida,
Póne reprendit pállio, resupínat: respició, rogo
Quam ób rem retineát me; ait esse uétitum intro ad
eram accédere.
'Sóphrona modo frátrem huc' inquit 'sénis introduxít
Chremem'; 865
Éumque nunc esse íntus cum illis. Hóc ubi ego
audiui, ád fores
Súspenso gradú placide ire pérrexi, accessi, ádstiti,
Ánimam compressi, aúrem admoui; ita ánimum coepi
atténdere,
Hóc modo sermónem captans.

PH. Eú, Geta!

GE. Hic pulcérrimum
Fácinus audiui; ítaque paene hercle éxclamaui
gaúdio. 870

AN. Quód?

GE. Quodnam arbitráre?

AN. Nescio.

GE. Átqui mirificíssumum:
Pátruos tuos est páter inuentus Phánio, uxorí tuae.

AN. Quíd aïs?

GE. Cum eius consuéuit olim mátre in Lemno
clánculum.

PH. Sómnium: utin haec ígnoraret súom patrem?

GE. Aliquid crédito,
Phórmio, esse caúsae; sed men cénses potuisse
ómnia 875
Íntellegere extra óstium, intus quae ínter sese ipsi
égerint?

AN. Átque ego quoque inaúdiui illam fábulam.

GE. Immo etiám dabo,

Quó magis credas: pátruos interea índe huc egreditúr foras;
Haúd multo post cúm patre idem récipit se intro dénuo:
Áït uterque tíbi potestatem éius adhibendaé dari. 880
Dénique ego sum míssus, te ut requírerem atque addúcerem.

AN. Quín ergo rape mé; quid cessas?
GE. Fécero.
AN. O mi Phórmio,
Vále!
PH. Vale, Antiphó!
AN. Bene, ita me dí ament, factum:
PH. Gaúdeo.

PHORMIO

Tantám fortunam de ínprouiso esse hís datam!
Summa éludendi occásiost mihi númc senes 885
Et Phaédriae curam ádimere argentáriam,
Ne quoíquam suorum aequálium suppléx siet.
Nam idem hóc argentum ita út datumst ingrátiis
Ei dátum erit; hoc qui cógam, re ipsa répperi.
Nunc géstus mihi uoltúsque est capiundús nouos. 890
Sed hínc concedam in ángiportum hoc próxumum
Inde hísce ostendam me, úbi erunt egressí foras.
Quo me ádsimularam ire ád mercatum, nón eo.

DEMIPHO CHREMES PHORMIO
Senes II *Parasitvs*

DE. Dis mágnas merito grátias habeo átque ago,
Quando éuenere haec nóbis, frater, próspere. 895
CH. Estne íta uti dixi líberalis?
DE. Óppido.
Quantúm potest, nunc cónueniundust Phórmio,
Prius quám dilapidat nóstras trigintá minas

Vt aúferamus.

PH. Démiphonem sí domist

Visam, út quod...

DE. At nos ád te ibamus, Phórmio. 900

PH. De eadem hác fortasse caúsa?

DE. Ita hercle.

PH. Crédidi:

Quid ád me ibatis?

DE. Rídiculum.

PH. An uerebámini,

Ne nón id facerem, quód recepissém semel?

Heus, quántaquanta haec méa paupertas ést, tamen

Adhúc curaui unum hóc quidem, ut mi essét fides. 905

Idque ádeo uenio núntiatum, Démipho,

Parátum me esse: ubi uóltis, uxorém date.

Nam omnís posthabui míhi res, ita uti pár fuit,

Postquam íd tanto opere uós uelle animaduérteram.

DE. At hic déhortatus ést me, ne illam tíbi darem: 910

'Nam quí erit rumor pópuli' inquit, 'si id féceris!

Olím quom honeste pótuit, tum non ést data;

Eam núnc extrudi túrpest.' Ferme eadem ómnia,

Quae túte dudum córam me incusáueras.

PH. Satís superbe inlúditis me.

DE. Quí?

PH. Rogas? 915

Quia ne álteram quidem íllam potero dúcere;

Nam quó redibo ore ád eam, quam contémpserim?

CH. 'Tum autem Ántiphonem uídeo ab sese amíttere

Inuítum eam' inque.

DE. Tum aútem uideo fílium

Inuítum sane múlierem ab se amíttere. 920

Sed tránsi sodes ád forum atque illúd mihi

Argéntum rursum iúbe rescribi, Phórmio.

PH. Quodne égo discripsi pórro illis, quibus débui?

DE. Quid ígitur fiet?

PH. Sí uis mi uxorém dare,

Quam déspondisti, dúcam; sin est, út uelis 925

Manére illam apud te, dós hic maneat, Démipho.

Nam nón est aequom mé propter uos décipi,

Quom ego uéstri honoris caúsa repudium álterae

Remíserim, quae dótis tantundém dabat.

DE. In' ín malam rem hinc cum ístac magnificéntia, 930

Fugitíue? Etiam nunc crédis te ignorárier

Aut túa facta adeo?

PH. Inrítor.

DE. Tune hanc dúceres,

Si tíbi daretur?

PH. Fác periclum.

DE. Vt fílius

Cum illa hábitet apud te: hoc uéstrum consiliúm fuit.

PH. Quaesó, quid narras?

DE. Quín tu mi argentúm cedo. 935

PH. Immo uéro uxorem tú cedo.

DE. In ius ámbula!

PH. Enimuéro si porro ésse odiosi pérgitis...

DE. Quid fácies?

PH. Egone? Vós me indotatís modo

Patrócinari fórtasse arbitrámini;

Etiám dotatis sóleo.

CH. Quid id nostrá?

PH. Nihil. 940

Hic quándam noram, quoíus uir uxorem...

CH. Hém.

DE. Quid est?

PH. ...Lemni hábuit aliam,
CH. Núllus sum.
PH. ex qua fíliam
Suscépit; et eam clam éducat.
CH. Sepúltus sum.
PH. Haec ádeo ego illi iám denarrabo.
CH. Óbsecro,
Ne fácias.
PH. Oh, tune ís eras?
DE. Vt ludós facit! 945
CH. Missúm te facimus.
PH. Fábulae.
CH. Quid uís tibi?
Argéntum, quod habes, cóndonamus te.
PH. Aúdio.
Quid uós malum ergo mé sic ludificámini
Inépti uestra púerili inconstantia?
Noló, uolo; uolo, nólo rursum; cápe, cedo; 950
Quod díctum, indictumst; quód modo erat ratum, ínritumst.
CH. Quo pácto aut unde hic haéc resciuit?
DE. Néscio;
Nisi mé dixisse némini certó scio.
CH. Monstri, íta me di ament, símile.
PH. Inieci scrúpulum.
DE. Hem,
Hicíne ut a nobis hóc tantum argenti aúferat 955
Tam apérte inridens? Émori hercle sátius est.
Animó uirili praésentique ut sís para:
Vidés tuom peccátum esse elatúm foras
Neque iam íd celare pósse te uxorém tuam.
Nunc quód ipsa ex aliis aúditura sít, Chreme, 960

Id nósmet indicáre placabílius est;
Tum hunc ínpuratum póterimus nostró modo
Vlcísci.

PH. Attat, nísi mi prospicio, haéreo.
Hi gládiatorio ánimo ad me adfectánt uiam.

CH. At uéreor, ut placári possit.

DE. Bóno animo es: 965
Ego rédigam uos in grátiam, hoc fretús, Chreme,
Quom e médio excessit, únde haec susceptást tibi.

PH. Itane ágitis mecum? Sátis astute adgrédimini.
Non hércle ex re istius me ínstigasti, Démipho.
Ain tu? úbi, quae lubitum fúerit, peregre féceris 970
Neque huíus sis ueritus féminae primáriae,
Quin nóuo modo eï fáceres contuméliam,
Veniás nunc precibus laútum peccatúm tuom?
Hisce égo illam dictis íta tibi incensám dabo,
Vt né restinguas, lácrumis si exstilláueris. 975

DE. Tantáne adfectum quémquam esse hominem audácia!
Non hóc publicitus scélus hinc asportárier 978
In sólas terras!

CH. Ín id redactus súm loci,
Vt quíd agam cum illo nésciam prorsum.

DE. Égo scio: 980
In iús eamus!

PH. Ín ius? Huc, si quíd lubet.

CH. Adséquere, retine, dúm ego huc seruos éuoco.

DE. Enim néqueo solus: áccurre.

PH. Vna iniúriast
Tecúm.

DE. Lege agito ergo.

PH. Álterast tecúm, Chreme.

CH. Rape húnc.

PH. Sic agitis? Énim uero uocést opus: 985
Nausístrata, exi!
CH. Os ópprime: inpurúm uide
Quantúm ualet.
PH. Nausístrata! inquam.
DE. Nón taces?
PH. Taceám?
DE. Nisi sequitur, púgnos in uentrem íngere.
PH. Vel óculum exsculpe: est úbi uos ulciscár probe.

NAVSISTRATA CHREMES DEMIPHO PHORMIO
Mvlier *Senes II* *Parasitvs*

NA. Qui nóminat me? Hem, quíd istuc turbaest, óbsecro,
Mi uír?
PH. Ehem, quid nunc óbstipuisti?
NA. Quís hic homost? 991
Non míhi respondes?
PH. Hícine ut tibi respóndeat,
Qui hercle úbi sit nescit?
CH. Cáue isti quicquam créduis.
PH. Abi, tánge; si non tótus friget, me énica.
CH. Nihil ést.
NA. Quid ergo? quíd istic narrat?
PH. Iám scies: 995
Auscúlta.
CH. Pergin crédere?
NA. Quid ego óbsecro
Huic crédam, qui nihil díxit?
PH. Delirát miser
Timóre.
NA. Non pol témerest, quod tu tám times.
CH. Egon tímeo?

PH. Recte sáne: quando níhil times,
Et hoc níhil est, quod ego díco, tu narrá.
DE. Scelus, 1000
Tibi nárret?
PH. Ohe tu, fáctumst abs te sédulo
Pro frátre.
NA. Mi uir, nón mihi dices?
CH. Át...
NA. Quid 'at'?
CH. Non ópus est dicto.
PH. Tíbi quidem; at scito huíc opust:
In Lémno
DE. Hem, quid aïs?
CH. Nón taces?
PH. clam te
CH. Eí mihi!
PH. Vxórem duxit.
NA. Mí homo, di meliús duint! 1005
PH. Sic fáctumst.
NA. Perii mísera.
PH. Et inde fíliam
Suscépit iam unam, dúm tu dormis.
CH. Quíd agimus?
NA. Pro di ímmortales, fácinus miserandum ét malum!
PH. Hoc áctumst.
NA. An quicquam hódiest factum indígnius? 1009
Qui mi, úbi ad uxores uéntumst, tum fiúnt senes!
Démipho, te appéllo; nam cum hoc ípso distaedét loqui:
Haécine erant itiónes crebrae et mánsiones díutinae
Lémni? Haecine erat éa, quae nostros mínuit fructus, uílitas?

DE. Égo, Nausistrata, ésse in hac re cúlpam meritum nón nego;
Séd ea quin sit ígnoscenda...

PH. Vérba fiunt mórtuo. 1015

DE. Nám neque neclegéntia tua néque odio id fecít tuo.
Vínolentus fére abhinc annos quíndecim muliérculam
Éam compressit, únde haec natast; néque postilla umquam áttigit.
Éa mortem obiit, é medio abiit, quí fuit in re hac scrúpulus.
Quam ób rem te oro, ut ália facta túa sunt, aequo animo hóc feras. 1020

NA. Quíd ego aequo animo? Cúpio misera in hác re iam defúngier;
Séd quid sperem? aetáte porro mínus peccaturúm putem?
Iám tum erat senéx, senectus sí uerecundós facit.
Án mea forma atque aétas nunc magis éxpetendast, Démipho?
Quíd mi hic adfers, quam ób rem exspectem aut spérem porro nón fore? 1025

PH. Éxsequias Chreméti quibus est cómmodum ire, em, témpus est!
Síc dabo: age nunc Phórmionem quí uolet lacéssito:
Fáxo tali sít mactatus átque hic est infortúnio.
Rédeat sane in grátiam iam: súpplici satis ést mihi.
Hábet haec, eï quód, dum uiuat, úsque ad aurem oggánniat. 1030

NA. Át meo merito crédo. Quid ego núnc commemorem. Démipho,
Síngulatim, quális ego in hunc fúerim?

DE. Noui aeque ómnia

Técum.

NA. Merito hoc méo uidetur fáctum?

DE. Minime géntium.

Vérum iam, quando áccusando fíeri infectum nón potest,

Ígnosce: orat, cónfitetur, púrgat: quid uis ámplius?

PH. Énimuero prius quam haéc dat ueniam, míhi prospiciam et Phaédriae. 1036

Héus Nausistratá, prius quam huic respóndes temere, audí!

NA. Quid est?

PH. Égo minas trigínta per falláciam ab illoc ábstuli:

Éas dedi tuo gnáto; is pro sua amíca lenoní dedit.

CH. Hém, quid aïs?

NA. Adeón indignum hoc tíbi uidetur, fílius 1040

Hómo adulescens sí habet unam amícam, tu uxorés duas?

Níhil pudere? quo óre illum obiurgábis? Respondé mihi.

DE. Fáciet, ut uolés.

NA. Immo ut meam iám scias senténtiam,

Néque ego ignosco néque promitto quícquam neque respóndeo,

Príus quam gnatum uídero; eius iudício permitto ómnia: 1045

Quód is iubebit fáciam.

PH. Mulier sápiens es, Nausístrata.

NA. Sátin tibist?

DE. Ita.

CH. Ímmo uero púlcre discedo ét probe

Ét praeter spem.

NA. Tú tuom nomen díc mihi quid sit.

PH. Phórmio:
Vostrae familiae hércle amicus ét tuo summus Phaédriae.
NA. Phórmio, at ego ecástor posthac tíbi, quod potero, quód uoles 1050
Fáciamque et dicám.
PH. Benigne dícis.
NA. Pol meritúmst tuom.
PH. Vín primum hodie fácere quod ego gaúdeam Nausístrata,
Ét quod tuo uiro óculi doleant?
NA. Cúpio.
PH. Me ad cenám uoca!
NA. Pól uero uoco.
PH. Eámus intro hinc!
NA. Fíat! Sed ubist Phaédria,
Iúdex noster?
PH. Iam híc faxo aderit. Ω. Vós ualete et plaúdite! 1055

TABLE OF METRES

1–152, iambic senarii.
153, 154, trochaic octonarii.
155, trochaic septenarius.
156, iambic septenarius.
157, trochaic octonarius.
158, 159, trochaic septenarii.
160–162, iambic octonarii.
163, iambic quaternarius.
164–176, iambic octonarii.
177, 178, iambic septenarii.
179, trochaic octonarius.
180, trochaic septenarius.
181, 182, iambic octonarii.
183, iambic quaternarius.
184, iambic octonarius.
185, trochaic septenarius.
186, iambic octonarius.
187, 188, trochaic octonarii.
189, 190, trochaic septenarii.
191, iambic quaternarius.
192, 193, iambic octonarii.
194, iambic senarius.
195, iambic octonarius.
196, iambic quaternarius.
197–215, trochaic septenarii.
216–230, iambic senarii.
231, 232, trochaic septenarii.
233–251, iambic octonarii.
252, 253, trochaic septenarii.
254–314, iambic senarii.
315–347, trochaic septenarii.
348–464, iambic senarii.
465–468, trochaic octonarii.
469, 470, trochaic septenarii.
471–478, iambic octonarii.
479, 480, trochaic octonarii.
481, 482, trochaic septenarii.
483, iambic octonarius.
484, trochaic septenarius.
485, trochaic binarius.
486, iambic octonarius.
487–489, trochaic septenarii.
490, iambic senarius.
491, iambic septenarius.
492, iambic octonarius.
493–495, trochaic septenarii.
496, iambic octonarius.
497–501, trochaic septenarii.
502, 503, iambic octonarii.
504–566, trochaic septenarii.
567–712, iambic senarii.
713–727, iambic octonarii.
728, trochaic octonarius.
729, trochaic quaternarius.
730, 731, trochaic octonarii.
732, trochaic septenarius.
733, 734, iambic octonarii.
735–738, trochaic octonarii.
739–741, trochaic septenarii.
742–747, iambic octonarii.
748–794, iambic septenarii.
795–819, iambic octonarii.
820–827, iambic septenarii.
829–840, iambic octonarii.
841–883, trochaic septenarii.
884–1010, iambic senarii.
1011–1055, trochaic septenarii.

NOTES

The Didascalia

These διδασκαλίαι are traditional accounts of the original performances of these plays. The present one may be translated thus:

'Here begins the Phormio of Terence, acted at the Roman Games under the curule aedileship of Lucius Postumius Albinus and Lucius Cornelius Merula. The manager was Lucius Ambivius Turpio with Lucius Atilus of Palestrina. Music composed by Flaccus, slave of Claudius, for flutes, bass and treble throughout. The play from "The Claimant," a Greek play of Apollodorus. The author's fourth play, composed in the consulship of Gaius Fannius and Marcus Valerius.'

Ludis Romanis. Held in September in honour of Jupiter. They included races in the Circus Maximus and dramatic performances.

The curule aediles superintended the public games.

Apollodoru, Ἀπυλλοδώρου, genitive case.

Coss. The year is B.C. 161.

Personae

The names in this play seem to have been all genuine names of inhabitants of Athens, and we can hardly even say that they were chosen for any supposed appropriateness. The name of Phormio is said to have been a normal stage-name for an adventurer, but it was the name of the great Admiral in the Peloponnesian War. Antipho the orator, Cratinus the comedian, and Crito the friend of Socrates were well-known personages of a former age. The slaves take their names from the country of their origin. The Dacians and the Getans were perhaps the same people, or at any rate were closely akin and spoke the same tongue, a fact to which Davus alludes in the opening lines of the play. Several of the names figure in other plays. In fact they were always in stock, like the Lovels and the Beverleys of our eighteenth century comedies, and the names which figure again and again in the Venetian comedies of Goldoni.

PROLOGUE

The prologues of Terence bear some resemblance to the parabasis of the earliest Athenian comedies. The dramatist defends himself and attacks his dispraisers.

1. postquam is here causal.

poeta uetus. Luscius Lanuvinus, whose comedies are not extant. There is a slight sneer in the epithet, which implies that Terence set a better fashion.

poetam. Terence never mentions himself by name.

5. oratione, scriptura. The one word seems to refer to the language, the other to the subject-matter. Terence's translations were simple and clear in style and he chose plays which had no strained and unnatural incidents such as his rival preferred.

7. ceruam fugere: the object of *uidere*.

9. stetit. The opposite word is *cecidit*, 'failed.'

10. actoris, i.e. the chief actor and manager.

11. laedit, i.e. with words, 'hits at him,' 'traduces him.'

15. haberet cui male diceret, 'had someone to abuse.'

16. in medio, ἐν μέσῳ, 'open to all.'

17. artem musicam, τὴν μουσικήν; properly used of all intellectual studies or occupations but here limited to the drama.

20. audisset bene, καλῶς ἂν ἤκουσε, 'should have been well spoken of,' cf. 359. The Romans, like some modern speakers of English, do not readily distinguish the senses of 'should' and 'would.'

23. quom, 'although.' The use of the word in this sense with the indicative survived colloquially and is found in Cicero's letters.

26. hic, 'the present dramatist.'

32. grex, 'troupe' of actors.

motus loco. This is said to refer to the failure of the Hecyra, Mother in Law, an earlier comedy of Terence's.

ACT I, SCENE I

The scene is probably a carfax or juncture of four streets at Athens, where are the houses of Chremes, Demipho, and Dorio. Davus enters carrying a small money-bag.

35. amicus summus meus et popularis. This would be a natural phrase in the mouth of an Athenian gentleman, the last word being δημότης or possibly φυλέτης. Slaves imitate the language of their masters.

Davus is a Dacian and it would seem that the Dacians and the Getans were identified.

37. relicuom seems to have been four syllables down to Imperial times.

38. id ut conficerem. The phrase follows *uenit* above, the sentence between being parenthetic, and we must understand *orans* or *rogans* as in 404 below.

39. erilem filium, 'his master's son.' The use of the adjective for the genitive of the noun is common in Greek, and the original words may have been *δεσποτικὸν υἱόν*. Cf. 104, *paternum amicum*.

40. conraditur, 'is scraping together.' The word is colloquial and hardly used except, as here, of money.

41. comparatum. The usual word for the arrangements of life.

ei qui.... The phrase is put before *ut* in colloquial emphasis, cf. 66.

43. demenso. The slave's *diaria* or daily allowance of food was so scanty that but little could be saved from it.

44. genium. The original word was probably *ψυχήν*, appetite. A man's *genius* in this limited sense was his desire of and capacity for enjoyment.

45. illa refers back to *uxorem*.

46. quanto labore partum. To understand *sit* is not natural and indeed hardly possible. The verb must be understood from the foregoing sentence and is therefore *abripiat*, while *partum* is not nominative but accusative.

47. ferietur. So an Englishman might say that he had been hit for a wedding present, but the Latin regards the present as the missile.

49. ubi initiabunt. The warning here cannot at present be ascertained. We do not know what the initiation was nor whether it took place on the birthday. We cannot therefore say whether there is a reference to a third gift or a further description of the occasion of the second.

50. causa, *πρόφασις*, 'pretext.'

mittundi. In this usage the verb loses all sense of sending and is used of making a present even when the giver takes it in person. The usage, originally colloquial and put by Virgil into the mouth of a shepherd, was normal in the Silver Age.

uideon. We might say 'don't I see?' The use of *nonne* was not fully established in Terence's time.

ACT I, SCENE 2

Geta comes out of Demipho's house and speaks down the passage (*uestibulum*) to a slave within.

52. em is the clipt imperative of *emo*, of which the original sense was 'take.' We might render 'here you are.'

53. lectum. Counterfeit and clipt coins seem to have been common at Athens.

conueniet. The tense implies that the statement will be found to be true. Thus *sic erit* means 'You will find it so.' This is still the regular sense of the Italian *sarà*. In Scotland a like idiom is found especially in questions with an affirmative form, as 'You'll be Mr Macfarlane?' cf. 801.

numerus quantum debui. The phrase is elliptical. He means 'the number of coins will tally with the account which I owed.'

54. amo te is a formula of returning thanks: cf. 478.

non neclexisse. The accusative subject can be understood in conversation and in poetry when there is no doubt what it must be; cf. 205. The construction of the accusative and infinitive after *habeo gratiam* seems to be colloquial.

55. adeo res redit, 'things are come to such a pass.'

redit. Like contracted forms of the perfect were perhaps common colloquially. Virgil has *petit* as a perfect. The prefix *red-* was apt to lose the sense of 'back' and imply merely a change, as in our 'reduce' and the like. Cf. 153, 317.

58. quĭd ĭstŭc ĕst was probably pronounced as one word with the stress on the penultimate.

59. modo ut tacere possis. It seems incorrect to take *modo ut* as equivalent to *dummodo*. Rather *ut* has the sense of *utinam* and *modo ut* would be represented in English by 'I only wish that....' Thus in And. 409, when the young man is told to keep his head, he says *modo ut possim*, 'I only wish I could,' cf. 773 below. At this time *utinam* was supplanting *ut* with an optative verb, but *ut* remained in a few set phrases, as *ut te di perdant* and probably, as here, with *modo*.

abi is colloquial like our 'go along with you,' and Shakespeare's 'go to.' Since however the original implication was 'your presence is no longer necessary,' it could mean 'you have done all that was wanted,' and in that case was used to express approval, like our 'well done' or 'bravo.'

sis = *si uis*, 'if you please.' According to the tone it modifies or, as here, emphasizes a command.

60. perspexeris. The subjunctive is causal.

61. uerba credere, 'to entrust a story.'

ubi, 'and that in case where.'

64. quid ni? lit. 'why not?' or 'how not?' but equivalent to our 'of course.' The word *ni* as a simple negative died out.

quid? The word is used to introduce a new instance or point like our 'again.' Here we might render it by 'and.'

67. hospitem. *ξένον*, a friend in a foreign country, a foreigner.

antiquom. In later Latin this word usually means 'existing of old' and *uetus* 'existing from of old,' but in Terence *uetus* usually means 'old in years' or 'worn out.'

68. modo non, *ὅσον οὐ*, lit. so much as just not to be, i.e. 'all but.'

montis auri is like the Highlander's 'Ben Lomond's of sneechan,' i.e. snuff.

69. desinas. The use of the present subjunctive for a command to a definite person died out in Latin. Its use in a general command survived.

70. regem me esse oportuit. Since the fourth century the words have been explained to mean 'It is *I* that should have been the rich man,' with the implication that the speaker would have been content with great and would not have aimed at superfluous riches. To this interpretation two objections may be offered. (i) The words should then have been *me regem*, not *regem me*. (ii) The word *rex*, though used by Plautus for a great or fortunate man and by Terence for the patron of a parasite, has not elsewhere in Terence that sense of a rich man or a millionaire which afterwards became so common. Here the natural meaning of the words seems to be 'It's a king I should have been,' with the implication that he would then not have allowed anyone to have more than a certain income, say ten thousand a year.

72. prouinciam in its original sense of a sphere of duty.

74. memini relinqui me. When used of personal experience *memini* usually takes the present infinitive to show the vividness of the remembrance.

deo irato meo: ablative absolute. Misfortunes were attributed to the god who was the sufferer's patron or to the gods in general. Thus *natus dis iratis* is equivalent to our 'born under an unlucky star.'

76. dum sum does not mean 'so long as I was' but is an equivalent for the lost present participle and gives a reason, cf. 768.

scapulas perdidi, 'I ruined my shoulder-blades,' which were the whipping-spot of his master's stick.

77. istaec: probably fem. pl. but possibly neuter.

78. calces, sc. *iactare*. The Greek proverb is πρὸς κέντρα μὴ λάκτιζε, 'don't kick against the goads.' The goad is used in driving oxen and an ox can do little mischief with his heels, so that by kicking he only brings more pricks upon him. Thus the phrase became proverbial for useless opposition.

79. uti foro, ἀγορᾷ χρῆσθαι, properly to get supplies but metaphorically of doing the best for oneself.

80. nil quicquam, 'nothing at all,' an emphatic pleonasm. The verb understood is *fecit*.

hic is contemptuous, 'Master Phaedria.'

84. quod daretur, i.e. he had no money to buy her.

85. oculos pascere. The singer in Shakespeare tells us that fancy, i.e. unsubstantial love, 'is engender'd in the eyes, By gazing fed.'

86. ludum, sc. *fidicinum*, 'the music school.'

87. nos, i.e. his master and himself.

88. ilico, 'directly' (*in loco*).

89. tonstrina. At Athens and Rome, as in Medieval Italy, the barber's shop served the purpose of our clubs.

fere plerumque. The pleonasm seems to be slave's language.

91. interea, 'one day.' Cf. 860, 878.

illi is the locative like our 'there.'

92. mirarier: historic infinitive : cf. 96 etc.

93. quid sit, 'what's the matter.'

94. uisum. Participles and pronouns are regularly attracted to the gender of the complement.

95. hic uiciniae. The case is probably locative.

96. miseram goes with *uirginem*.

97. sita erat, προὔκειτο. The body in accordance with Athenian law was laid out in a ground-floor room. The Latin name for this lying-in-state was *collocatio*.

99. miseritumst, sc. *me*.

101. commorat for *commouerat.*

ibi, 'thereupon.'

102. uoltisne eamus? This must have been the original construction with *uolo* when there is a change of person, and it survived colloquially and in poetry. In formal prose *ut* was inserted before the subjunctive.

eamus uisere. This was an original use of the infinitive which, as in origin a dative, could express purpose. It survived colloquially and in the poets with verbs of motion and with *do* and some of its compounds.

alius may stand for *alter* and refer to Phaedria but it may mean some other young man who was of the party.

103. sodes = *si audes*, 'if you please.' The earlier meaning of *audeo* (*auideo* from *auidus*) is desire.

uenimus, 'we are come.' The change of tense is vivid and natural.

104. quo magis diceres. This is not the common final construction with *quo* and a comparative. The verb is potential and the antecedent of the relative *quo* is the sentence which follows, *nil aderat*, etc. We should say 'to make you say it the more.'

107. uis seems here to mean a quantity, as in Virgil's *odora canum uis* and Horace's *hederae uis.*

110. satis, 'fairly.'

scita, 'pretty,' a colloquial sense of the word.

111. scin quam would in full be *scisne quam amare coeperit* but is used without thought of the full construction. The phrase is almost slang and may be rendered 'Rather!' It is also used in threats with the sense of the countryman's 'I'll larn you!'

euadat. The subject is Antipho, 'See to what a length he goes, cf. 626. The verb cannot be impersonal.

113. faciat copiam, 'allow him to visit her.'

enim. In this sense of 'indeed' the word died out except as an archaism in heroic poetry: cf. 332.

114. neque enim aequom ait facere. Since the negative is part of the reported speech and the conjunction is not, *neque* is here used for *et non*, as it is often by Livy and sometimes by Cicero.

117. quid ageret, 'what line to take.'

119. daret, ἐδίδου ἄν, 'had been for giving.'

122. quid fiat? A question repeated by the person to whom it is put, takes both in Greek and in Latin the indirect form. The repetition usually expresses either surprise or vexation.

parasitus. The word means literally one who dines with others and was first applied to a class of officials who assisted the priests at Athens. By a jest of Alexis, a comedian of the fourth century, it was transferred to men who live, as the phrase is, by their wits, getting invitations to dinner by flattery or by services which were beneath a gentleman. Probably the character, like the Pykes and Plucks, was more frequent in comedy than in life, but no doubt there were such men.

123. confidens in this colloquial sense of 'impudent' or 'brazen' did not survive but was once put by Virgil into the mouth of the rather boorish Proteus: *Namquis te, iuuenum confidentissime, nostras | iussit adire domos?*

qui, like *ut*, is an old pronominal ablative and like *ut* is used with an optative verb. Sometimes *ut qui* are used together in the same way. All the three, *ut*, *qui*, and *ut qui* were supplanted in this use by *utinam*.

perduint is an optative form parallel with *uelint*, *edint*, etc. and afterwards supplanted by *perdant* which was formed on the analogy of *regant*. All these were used as subjunctives.

125. lex. By this law of Solon's the next of kin had the choice of marrying the girl or providing her with a dowry.

127. scribam dicam, γράψομαι δικήν, 'I will bring an action.' The pure Latin phrase was *litem inferre.*

129. qui. The use of *qui* as an indirect interrogative, a common use in the comedians, seems never to have become obsolete. As a direct interrogative *qui* survived only in poetry and then usually with the sense of *qualis*. The indirect use occurs below in 355 and the direct in 911, 990.

130. qui, 'how.'

131. quod. The antecedent is the understood object of *uincam* below: 'I shall carry any point which' etc.

133. lites in the sense of 'a row' is of the nature of slang: cf. 219.

mea, sc. *refert*, 'what does it matter to me?' cf. 389, 723, 800, 940.

134. iocularem audaciam! 'a sporting venture!'

137. te is the instrumental ablative found also with *facio* and *fio* and like our 'what's to be done with him?' though with 'become' our preposition is 'of.' Cf. *illa quid futurumst*, 811.

138. aequo animo. The slave assumes the style of a Stoic philosopher.

141. amitte, 'let him off,' a sense of the word found also in Cicero and Caesar.

142. quicquam, sc. *admiserit*, 'if he sin again.'

nil, *οὐδέν*, is adverbial, like the old English 'nothing afraid.'

143. uel, 'if you like.' The word is the athematic imperative of *uelle*. Cf. 989.

144. paedagogus was the slave who took children to school. Here it is applied in jest to Phaedria on account of Geta's *ducere et redducere* in l. 86 and *ducit et redducit* are understood with *citharistriam*. The jest is marred if we understand *amat* or *sectatur*.

148. quoad exspectatis, 'until when are you waiting,' i.e. 'when do you expect.'

150. portitores, *τοὺς τελώνας*, the custom-house officers, who seem to have had the right of opening letters from abroad.

151. num quid aliud me uis? lit. 'have you anything else to ask of me?' a common formula of leave-taking: cf. 458.

152. hoc is an alternative form of *huc*, both being accusatives of *hic*, at first used indifferently but afterwards restricted, *huc* used for the accusative of the goal of motion and *hoc* for the direct object.

cape. He hands the bag to the slave who comes to the door. Dorcium is Geta's wife. After this act a minute or so elapses.

ACT II, SCENE I

The cousins enter from Demipho's.

153, 154. The order of the words and the repetition of *ut* show the speaker's agitation.

adeon rem redisse. The accusative and infinitive in an exclamatory question is the object of an unexprest thought or feeling. Here the feeling is vexation or regret. The question can be used with or without *ne*. Cf. 884.

154. aduenti. The genitive forms in *-us* were eschewed in common speech and by some men of letters. The case here follows *ueniat in mentem* which takes the construction usual with *memini*.

155. fuissem of past time, **exspectarem** of present, the normal use of the tenses in hypothesis and conditional statement.

ut par fuit. Our idiom, less logical, says 'as would have been right.' So *melius fuit* and other like expressions.

156. rogitas? In this use *rogas* or *rogitas* implies that the question just put is superfluous because the answer must be evident. We say 'How can you ask?' or 'What a question!' Cf. 574, 915.

157. quod in this use becomes a conjunction as in *quod si* and *quod ni*.

158. eo quod, 'to that step which.'

160. audio is an impatient exclamation, like our 'I know, I know!' Cf. 947.

161. quam mox. Although we may here say 'how soon,' the word *mox* never means 'soon' in the sense of 'within a brief time.' The usual word for 'soon' in that sense with a future verb is *iam*, as often in this play. The usual sense of *mox* is 'after an interval' or 'later on,' so here we might translate 'how long it will be before he comes.'

162. defit was supplanted in prose by *deficit*, but it probably survived in common speech as Virgil puts it into the mouth of a countryman.

162. dolet. This impersonal use is colloquial.

165. ita me di bene ament is followed by the indicative *cupio*. A like construction is found in Shakespeare's 'So come my soul to bliss as I speak true.' We more usually say 'May I be hanged if I do not desire.' Cf. 807.

ut mihi liceat, ἐφ' ᾧτε ἔξεσται, 'on condition that I be allowed,' or possibly the phrase is the object of *depecisci*, in which case the meaning is 'I am eager to buy at the price of my life the leave to enjoy' etc.

166. iam, 'at once.' Cf. 179 etc.

morte. In such a context we usually speak of giving one's life, the Romans of giving one's death.

168. ut ne addam. In negative final sentences it gradually became customary to drop the *ut*, so that *ne*, though it always means 'not,' seems at first sight to have a final sense. The use of *ut ne* never entirely disappeared.

171. quo. When the antecedent has a preposition, that preposition can be understood with the relative provided that the verb in both clauses is the same verb but not necessarily the same part of the verb.

sentias. This verb is especially used of unpleasant experience.

172. plerique omnes, 'almost all of us,' is a colloquial phrase.

nostri, though used as the genitive plural objective of *ego*, is etymologically the genitive of *noster* or *nostrum*. Possibly it is here the genitive of *nostrum* and in any case means 'our own lot.'

174. etiam, 'still.'

176. eius is the genitive after *amittendi* which is a noun substantive and is here used with the construction of a noun substantive. With this use the following genitive is almost always in the plural, but Terence once elsewhere has *eius uidendi*, where *eius* is feminine (Hec. 372). Usually the gerund is followed by the case used with the verb or with transitive verbs the gerundive is used.

ACT II, SCENE 2

Geta enters in much perturbation and does not at first see the young man.

179. nullus in the sense of 'ruined' is colloquial. Cf. 942.

celere in later Latin was displaced by *celeriter*.

180. inpendent. The verb is not found transitive after Terence's time.

183. illic is the pronoun.

184. tum is not temporal but means 'moreover' or perhaps rather 'what is worse,' a common sense of the word. Cf. 476, 918.

185. quod. The sense of the antecedent is to be found in *audacia* above.

186. laterem lauem. The proverb πλίνθον πλύνειν, to wash a brick, and the parallel λίθον ἕψειν, to boil a stone, are used of ineffectual labour. Washing does not take the colour out of a brick nor boiling soften a stone.

187. animi: locative case.

188. absque eo esset. Probably *que*, like the English 'an' for 'and,' means 'if.' Thus the literal meaning of the phrase is 'if it were apart from him,' i.e. 'if it were not for him.'

189. uidissem for *prouidissem* survived colloquially and is found in Cicero's letters.

190. protinam is a form due to false analogy with *palam*, *coram*, and the like, since *tenus* was originally a neuter noun and *protinus* meant 'a stretching forward.'

192. quaerere insistam. The use of *insisto* with an infinitive survived colloquially and is found in Cicero's letters.

193. hoc nuntio: abl. abs.

194. plurimum is used exactly as our 'mostly.'

195. satis pro imperio, lit. 'quite in accordance with supreme power,' i.e. 'pretty imperiously.' The verb understood is *loquere.* Geta has his back to Antipho and does not recognize the voice. Possibly the pitch-accent made Greek voices less easy to distinguish than ours. At any rate the failure to recognize a voice is a common incident in the comedies.

197. cedo. The former syllable is a demonstrative pronoun, seen in *hic*, *illic*, etc. and akin to our 'he' and 'here': the latter is the imperative of the verb *do*, supplanted by *da*, a form due to an attempt to bring the verb into the first conjugation. The word *cedo* means 'give here' or 'bring here' or 'say here.' In the sense of 'say' *do* is colloquial. It is put by Virgil into the mouth of a shepherd.

cedo quid portas. In early Latin an indirect question is often in the indicative especially, as here, after an imperative. Cf. 247, 358, 398, 798.

198. meumne? Antipho's fear makes him sure that Geta will understand him without his adding *patrem uidisti.* Phaedria being less directly interested does not catch the meanings.

intellexti = *intellexisti.*

hem: 'I say!'

203. fortis fortuna adiuuat. Menander's form of this proverb is τόλμῃ δικαίᾳ καὶ θεὸς συλλαμβάνει.

204. apud me, ἐντὸς ἐμαυτοῦ, 'in possession of my faculties.'

nunc quom maxume, 'now if ever.'

206. immutarier: middle voice.

208. hoc nihil est. The neuter seems to be used contemptuously of a person: 'This fellow's no good.'

ilicet, lit. 'you may go,' a formula used in dismissing a gathering, came to be used in the sense of 'all's over,' i.e. nothing more can be done.

209. quin abeo? A question with *quin* does not expect an answer and is in effect a command or a statement akin to a command. What Geta here says is 'there is no reason why I should not be off,' or rather 'let me be off.'

210. uoltum. In face of this word it is hard to believe that in Terence's time the actors wore masks.

212. istuc, 'that look.'

ut respondeas, ὅπως ἀποκρινεῖ, 'take care to answer.'

214. ui coactum te esse depends upon *ut respondeas*.

lege, iudicio, 'by the statute, by the judgment.'

215. in ultima platea, 'at the end of the street.'

220. plectar. The verb is especially used of vicarious or undeserved punishment. Antipho has got Geta into trouble.

pendens. A slave was hung up by the wrists in order that the flogging might be more effective.

223. mi: ethic dative. 'Don't talk to me of "oughts."'

quin tu impera, 'just give no orders.'

225. incipiunda. The usual meaning of this verb is, as here, 'to take in hand,' 'to undertake.' Cf. 710.

noxiam passes from the sense of 'harm' to that of 'blame.'

227. hem, 'very well.'

ACT II, SCENE 3

Demipho enters talking angrily to himself. He does not see the others.

231. itane tandem is used in questions of angry astonishment. Cf. 373, 413, 527.

232. mitto, ἐῶ, 'I say nothing of.'

234. monitor. Geta had been left in charge of Antipho, *quasi magister*.

uix tandem. Either 'he has mentioned me at last' or less probably 'I could hardly be called *monitor*.'

237. tradere, 'give away,' with the suggestion of treachery.

238. sine, 'leave it to me.'

242. aduorsam, 'when it faces them.'

243. pericla, 'law-suits.'

245. communia, 'that befall everybody.'

248. meditata: passive voice.

249. in pistrino. The grinding was done by hand and was very hard work.

250. opus, 'farm-work.' Cf. 363. The word for a farm-labourer was *opera*. A town-slave had an easy and interesting life.

255. saluom uenire.... Demea interrupts him before he can add *gaudeo*.

256. satine. Perhaps 'quite' is the commonest meaning of *saxis*.

257. uellem, 'I could have wished': potential for politeness.

259. id suscenses. The accusative of the inner object is most often, as here, a neuter pronoun. In English it survives in such phrases as 'go it.' With verbs of emotion it represents the cause, as here. Cf. 1052.

262. illum, 'of the past.'

267. tradunt operas mutuas, 'they assist one another in turn.'

270. est ut, 'it is the fact that.' This, and not 'it is possible that,' is always the meaning of the phrase. Cf. 925.

271. rei. Participial forms which have become adjectives have the genitive for their complement. Cf. 623.

272. quin = *qua ne*, 'why not.'

280. tua iusta, 'your rights,' i.e. the soundness of your case.

ubi, 'in a case where.'

281. functus. The verb was always transitive in early Latin and occasionally so in much later writers.

288. quoi = *cui*.

293. testimoni dictio. At Athens a slave could not be a witness except in a case of murder..

296. habere, 'to marry her.'

297. daretis, potential, 'you might have given,' or expressing duty, 'you ought to have given.'

298—9. ratione...ratio. Demipho uses the word in the sense of reason, Geta in that of reckoning. He could reckon the cost but not find the money.

299. sumeret, sc. *mutuom*, 'he should have borrowed it.'

300. alicunde is here, as often, an ablative form of *aliquis* and means 'from someone.' So under 'for whom,' etc. Cf. 333 etc.

302. siquidem quisquam crederet, 'yes, if anyone would have trusted him.' *Siquidem* is not used in the sense of *quasi*.

303. te uiuo. A young Athenian gentleman in Antipho's position would have no property of his own and therefore no money-lender would deal with him. A post-obit seems to have been unknown.

304. egon ut patiar. This is a normal form of an exclamatory question. Cf. 668, 874.

305. meritumst: passive voice.

308. faxo. This and other like forms seem to have been originally aorist subjunctive, which, like πράξω and the other parallel forms in Greek, came to be used as futures.

faxo hic aderit. In later Latin the phrase would have been *efficiam ut adsit*. Since *faxo aderit* is little more than a paraphrase for *aderit*, the colloquial phrase with the indicative is natural enough.

310. recta uia quidem illuc. These words are an aside to Geta and *illuc* means what Geta takes it to mean. Geta and Pamphila now go out.

311. deos penates. A Greek on his return home was bound to thank ἑστιούχους θεούς, the gods of the hearth, for his safe return.

313. amicos aduocabo. It will be remembered that the elder Mr Weller took a like course in his dealings with Mr Solomon Pell. 'Ve'll take a couple o' friends o' mine as'll wery soon be down upon him if he comes anythin' irreg'lar.' In fact, like Demipho, he took three.

adsient. The verb is technical of an *aduocatus*, one who assists a friend in a law-suit. Cf. 350.

ACT III, SCENE I

There has been a short interval. Now Geta returns with Phormio.

315. itane ais...? 'do you mean to tell me...?'

318. intristi=*intriuisti*. A favourite food with farm-labourers was a mixture of garlic, thyme, and other herbs bruised in a wooden salad-bowl. If the girl who made it made it badly, the man to whom she brought it would tell her to eat it herself as a punishment. Hence the proverb.

319—20. Phormio meditates and soliloquizes.

319. rogabit. See 379, 599.

320. reddet. The context shows that the meaning must be 'answers.'

321. corde. In early days the heart was supposed to be the seat of the intellect. Hence *cordatus homo*=an able man.

323. deriuem. Water was stored in reservoirs whence it could be let down into the fields by opening sluices.

325. neruom. We should say 'stocks' or 'pillory,' though we have long since ceased to use either. Cf. 696.

326. periclum. The same sense of 'trial' or 'experience' appears in *experior* and *peritus*. The sense of 'danger' is later. Cf. 933.

329. enumquam. The proclitic *en* emphasizes the question.

iniuriarum, 'assault and battery.'

330. Phormio had more ground for his comparison than young Macduff, who said to his mother 'Poor birds they are not set for.' Macbeth, IV. 2. 35.

tennitur. A colloquial form of *tenditur*.

332. in illis. Usually the word for 'the latter' is *hic*, for 'the former,' *ille*. If the text be right, Terence may have been influenced by the original τοῖς μὲν and τοῖς δὲ, but the awkwardness is very unlike him.

luditur, 'befooled,' because it is wasted.

334. ducent damnatum domum. A defendant who was cast in damages and failed to pay them might be claimed as a slave by the plaintiff.

338. regi, 'patron.' So βασιλεύς was used at Athens.

339. asymbolum. A dinner-party on the picnic principle where everyone contributes something seems to have been common at Athens. Sometimes the Romans adopted the custom, as when Horace proposes to contribute a jar of wine on condition that his friend brings a box of spikenard. The pure Latin word for *asymbolus* is *immunis*. When the dinner took place at an eating-house (cf. Eun. 608) the parasite's share of the cost was paid by his patron or divided among the guests.

340. ab animo. We say 'in mind' treating the mind as the seat, not as the source. Cf. *a fronte* and the like, *abs te* 840.

quom, 'whereas,' 'while.'

341. rideas. The word implies permission and the usage is akin to that of the subjunctive with *licet* as in 347.

342. decumbas. The Athenians, like the Romans, reclined at their meals.

343. istuc uerbi is hardly distinguishable from *istuc uerbum*. The genitive is one of specification and in this form is colloquial. Cf. 409, 815, 990.

dubites. The mood is consecutive. The dinner is of the kind to make you hesitate.

347. postilla was supplanted by *postea* before Cicero's time.

ACT III, SCENE 2

Demipho returns with three friends to whom he is talking.

350. adeste. See on 313.

hoc age, 'be attentive.' 'To be inattentive' is *aliud agere*. Cf. 435.

351. deum immortalium, sc. *fidem imploro*. Phormio pretends not to see Demipho and his friends. Geta makes the same pretence with the further one of wrath against Phormio.

359. male audies, 'you shall be called bad names.' Cf. 20.

362. minus is a mild negative.

grandior, 'oldish.'

363. opere. See on 250.

367. quem ego uiderim. This seems to be an instance of the restrictive subjunctive after a relative, a use hardly to be found elsewhere in early Latin with affirmative sentences except in the phrase *quod sciam*, 'as far as I know.'

368. uideas te atque illum narras, 'may you see yourself as you describe him,' i.e. you will never be *optimus*. The reading of the line is doubtful.

in malam crucem. Either *i* is understood or *in* stands for *isne*, in which case *malam crucem* is used like *domum* without a preposition. The curse, a common one, refers to the crucifixion of slaves. We ought perhaps to write *malamcrucem*, since the two words were pronounced as one with the stress on the antepenultimate. Cf. ἔρρε ἐς κόρακας.

371. quam. The antecedent is *hanc*, i.e. Phanium.

373. carcer. We say 'jail-bird,' but the Latin word is more forcible. In like manner the Duke in Henry VIII addresses Wolsey as 'thou scarlet sin.' Cf. *scelus*, 978, 1000.

374. extortor and **contortor** are the more effective for being nonce words.

377. numquam...hodie. Colloquially the word *hodie* with and occasionally even without a negative loses its temporal sense and merely emphasizes the negative or the whole statement. Cf. 626, 639, 805, 1009. As a colloquial phrase Virgil puts this *numquam hodie* into the mouth of a shepherd and into the mouth of an excited and desperate soldier.

379. potis. The word in early Latin is used of any gender and any number, as also in *pote*. Both forms died out, leaving a blank until a much later age invented the word *possibilis*.

380—1. explana qui...diceret. Normal Latin has no means of distinguishing what we express by 'Tell me what he was saying' and 'Tell me what he said.' For either sense *dixerit* is used. The use of *diceret* here is therefore difficult to explain. Possibly the mood is not due to this dependence on *explana* but is potential. In that case *qui diceret* means 'how he could say.'

386. perdidi, 'have let slip,' i.e. have forgotten. The speech is of course aside.

387. hem, 'look here.'

388. non dico. The use of the future for the present here is emphatic, like our 'I don't tell you.' Cf. 893. Often it is a mere colloquialism for the present, like our 'I start to-morrow' or 'I dine with the Smiths on Monday.' Cf. 446, 532, 893, etc.

389. Geta whispers the name.

atque adeo, 'and yet after all.'

392. horum. He points to Demipho's friends before whom a lie would be a special disgrace.

393. talentum. The old form of the genitive plural was already in most words supplanted by the later form in *-orum*. The property mentioned would be about £2500, but a man with such a property would be at least as well off as a man with six times the sum to-day.

394. memoriter never means 'by heart' but 'with exact memory,' 'without a mistake.'

esses...proferens = *proferres*. The form is analytic.

398. eu, noster, recte. This is said in pretended admiration to his master. The next words, if said aside to Phormio, imply that Demipho's argument wants care in the answering; if said aloud, they are a sham.

399. quibus me oportuit, sc. *expedire*.

400. fuerat. This is called the aorist pluperfect, being in sense an aorist with an emphasis on the past character of the act or state. Thus Propertius writes *non sum ego qui fueram*. Cf. 613, 651.

405. regnas, τυραννεύεις, 'are a despot.'

406. bis. There was no court of appeal at Athens. A case once decided could not be re-opened.

409—10. id.... In his vexation Demipho naturally breaks his sentences: *id dotis* depends upon *accipe* with *minas quinque* in apposition, while *abduce hanc* is thrown in between the two phrases, *id dotis* 'that amount of dowry.' See on 343.

418. at nos unde? sc. *proxime sumus*: lit. 'on what side are we next of kin?' We should say 'how are we next of kin?'

419. aiunt, 'as they say.' The saying quoted became proverbial, but, as it originally referred to a law-suit, it is specially applicable here.

426. tute idem melius feceris. The reading makes *idem* masculine emphasizing *tute*. If we read *tu te*, then *te* is ablative after *feceris*, and *idem* is neuter, but it may be doubted whether *idem* could stand here in the sense of *id ipsum*. Of course the suggestion that Demipho should turn out of his own house is merely abusive.

428. infelix from its original meaning of 'unfertile' came to mean 'calamitous' and seems here to be used as a term of reproach or abuse.

metuit. This and the next speech are whispers.

432. auditum uelim. It seems that there is no difference of meaning between an infinitive and a participle after *uolo*.

438. liberam, sc. *attingi*.

439. dicam tibi inpingam grandem, 'I'll hurl a law-suit at you with swingeing damages.'

440. me, sc. *arcesse*. Phormio sweeps off.

ACT III, SCENE 3

447. quid ago? a deliberative question. The subjunctive may be used with no difference of meaning. Thus we can say indifferently 'What do I do next?' and 'What am I to do next?' Cf. 812 etc.

Cratinum censeo. An infinitive is understood, as it might be in English.

451. restitui in integrum, 'be restored to its original position,' i.e. 'be null and void.'

458. fecistis probe is a formula of politeness, 'I am much obliged to you.' The next words are said after the departure of the *aduocati* and before Geta's return.

459. negant redisse, sc. *Antiphonem*.

464. eccum = *ecce hum*, i.e. *hunc* without the enclitic *-ce*.

in tempore, ἐν καιρῷ, 'in the nick.'

ACT III, SCENE 4

Antipho soliloquizes.

465. multimodis. Lexicons misled by the derivation give 'in many ways' as the meaning of this word. In the comedians it always means 'very' or 'very much.'

cum istoc animo. This usage of *cum* is common in comedy. Literally it means 'as accompanied by,' but it comes to have a causal sense. The verb with it is one of reproof, or abuse or reproof is implied. Cf. 930 and Eun. 153 *egon quicquam cum istis factis tibi respondeam?*

467. tete. The second syllable is long and the word is merely *te* doubled for emphasis. In *tutĕ* the second syllable is an enclitic particle.

468. utut stands to *quisquis* as *ut* to *quis* or *qui*. Cf. 904.

consuleres, 'you should have had thought.'

tuam fidem, τὴν σὴν πίστιν, 'her faith in you.' The use of the possessive pronoun for the objective genitive, though normal in Greek, is rare in Latin. Cf. 1016. In both instances Terence probably followed the Greek original.

469. ne quid poteretur. The use of *potior* with the accusative never quite died out but was eschewed by most writers.

471. qui abieris: causal subjunctive.

474. num quid patri subolet? The verb is impersonal and *quid* is the accusative of the inner object.

nil etiam, 'nothing as yet.'

475. nisi, 'only.' Cf. 953. The use is colloquial.

noui, καινοῦ, 'novel.'

476. strenuom hominem praebuit. Either *se* is understood or the phrase is like Ovid's *simularet anum* and our 'He has play'd the man.'

478. ego, sc. *feci* or *confutaui*.

quod potui. If the verb understood is *feci*, then *quod* is the object of *facere* also understood: if the verb is *confutaui* then *quod* is the accusative of the inner object and *quod potui* means 'as far as I could.'

480. quid eum? sc. *mansurus est*.

481. Strict grammar requires either *aibat sese velle* or *ut aibat uolt*. One sometimes hears in English such sentences as 'whom he said was come.'

482. metuis. This form of the genitive properly belonged to *ŭ* stems of the third declension but was occasionally used with *ŭ* stems of the fourth, whose proper genitive ended in *-ūs*.

saluom, sc. *venire*.

484. palaestra. This is a sneering jest. Phaedria has given up the usual daily visit to the gymnasium and goes to Pamphila's instead.

ACT III, SCENE 5

Dorio enters with an insolent air, Phaedria follows.

486. omitte me. Phaedria has clutcht hold of his sleeve.

490. mirabar si...adferres, lit. 'I was agape to see if you would bring,' i.e. 'I thought it would be a wonder if you were to bring,' or 'I wondered at your bringing,' like *ἐθαύμαζον εἰ*.

491. suo suat capiti, *ῥάπτει ἑαυτῷ*. The metaphor from stitching was a very old one. The meaning is not exactly 'be caught in his own trap,' but 'is setting a trap for himself.' The Latin uses the subjunctive whether what is feared be of the present or of the future, while the Greek, *δέδοικα μὴ ῥάπτει* and *δέδοικα μὴ ῥάπτῃ*, and the English, 'I fear he is' and 'I fear he will,' can make the distinction.

492. hariolare. It is clear that, when 'to speak as a soothsayer' came to mean 'to talk nonsense,' the Roman had lost his faith in the soothsayer's art.

493. faeneratum...pulcre, 'lent at a fine rate of interest.' The verb was deponent until post-Augustan times, but the participle is used passively, as is the case with many deponent verbs.

501. miseritumst, sc. *me eius*.

ueris uincor, i.e. 'I am beaten by the truth of his arguments.'

502. atque. This is Wagner's conjecture for *neque*. It is not very probable, but all attempts to give a reasonable sense to *neque* are failures and the true reading is yet to seek. If we read *atque*, then *alia sollicitudine* is used with much bitterness, 'another kind of uneasiness,' which is in fact no uneasiness at all but happiness, a happiness which Phaedria in his trouble grudges to his cousin.

503. quid istuc autem? He doesn't see what his cousin means.

504. domi may mean 'at your house' but at least suggests its other meaning 'in your possession.'

506–7. The Greek proverb is *τῶν ὤτων ἔχω τὸν λύκον· οὔτ' ἔχειν οὔτ' ἀφεῖναι δύναμαι.* The man cannot stand holding the wolf for ever and to let it go means death. There is a subtle syllepsis in *scio* which as applied to *amittam* refers to rational ability and as applied to *retineam* refers to physical ability. As a figure syllepsis is particularly applicable to something grim.

508. ne...sies. In later Latin this form of prohibition mostly gave way to *noli* with the infinitive except where the prohibition is general, where 'you' means 'any man,' as the 'thou' of the commandments.

511. indignum, lit. 'unfit,' hence 'scandalous.'

512. illo, i.e. the customer.

mutet fidem, 'break his word.'

513. triduom hoc go with *maneat.* Phaedria in his excitement becomes parenthetic.

515. optundes in the metaphorical sense of stun or deafen.

exoret sine. The imperative of *sino* is normally used with the simple subjunctive.

516. conduplicauerit. The force of the tense is 'you will certainly find that....' See further on 882.

519. neque ego neque tu. The two negatives, as often, imply a comparison: 'it will be no more my doing than yours,' with the implication that we all know that it is not yours.

quod es dignus. There seems no reason to suppose an ellipse. The neuter accusative of a pronoun might well be used with *dignus.* Plautus has *Non me censes scire quid dignus siem.*

521. contra. The word is usually an adv. in Terence, but this passage seems an early instance of its use as a preposition.

524. quam ad. A solitary instance in Terence of a monosyllabic preposition following its case.

526. vanitatis. The word *vanus* (lit. 'empty') means void of truth and honesty.

dum ob rem, sc. *sit,* 'provided it be to my interest.' The omission of the subjunctive verb is colloquial.

527. sic sum, 'that's my character.' The adverb, equivalent to an adjective, is the complement. So *aliter,* l. 530.

ACT III, SCENE 6

Dorio is gone. The rest remain.

535. si pote fuisset. The sense of the suppress apodosis is 'I should have had the money in time.'

536. promissum fuerat. This form of the pluperfect has here the sense of an emphatic aorist, 'was promised for certain.' See on 400.

537. qui me...adiuerit. We say 'when he helped me,' but the subjunctive is causal.

540. inuenias. The mood in the answer follows the subjunctive of the question.

542. etiam with an interrogative verb has the force of an impatient imperative. 'Just get along with you.'

544. quaerere in malo crucem. The equivalent English proverb speaks of the frying-pan and the fire.

549. tum igitur, 'in that case then.'

551. certumst, 'I am resolv'd.'

552. pedetemptim tamen. We have the same ellipse of the verb, 'But gently, Sir, gently.'

553. uide si quid...potes. The interrogative use of *si* and the subjunctive in the dependent question are colloquial.

555. malum is a slave's word for punishment, especially whipping.

559. o lepidum, sc. *caput*, 'you good soul!'

feres, *οἴσει*, 'you shall get.'

563. opera mea, 'my help.'

ACT IV, SCENE I

After a brief interval the two old gentlemen arrive from the Piraeus.

567. qua...filiam. In the full construction the antecedent of *qua causa* is *eam causam*, an accusative in apposition to the sentence *adduxtin tecum filiam.* The bringing home of his daughter is the motive which took him to Lemnos.

568. quid ita? *τί δαί;* 'why so?' This interrogative usually expresses surprise, sometimes reproach.

570. aetas. A Greek girl who did not marry young was not likely to find a husband at all.

571. ipsam...aibant. After the indicatives in the *postquam* clauses there would grammatically follow *ipsa profectast.* Slight changes of construction are common in conversation where some afterthought modifies the original intention.

574. pol me detinuit morbus. On the Westminster stage these words have been spoken 'with some confusion,' as though Chremes invented the illness to cover some other reason for his delay. For this explanation there seems to be no warrant. The position is this. Had Chremes returned at once, then in all probability he would have found the Lemnian wife and daughter, the wife would not have died, a marriage would have been arranged in the conventional way for Antipho and the daughter, and there would have been no play. The dramatist therefore was obliged to keep Chremes in Lemnos, and the most natural reason for such a detention was an illness. It follows that Chremes speaks not in confusion but in impatience. He is eager to get his brother's advice on his difficult position and cannot wait to tell his brother about an illness which is past and no longer of any consequence. The point is important because it shows that the dramatist, bound though he was to certain improbabilities by his unchanging scene and the conventionalities of his stage, nevertheless did his best to give probability to the incidents of his plot.

unde? 'how caught?'

580. sit. The subject is *illa*, 'the girl.'

584. opus est scito. The use of the perfect passive participle neuter for an abstract noun is most common after *opus*, but occurs even in the nominative, as in Virgil's *notumque furens quid femina possit*. So τὸ μέλλον = delay.

585. aliqua in later Latin gave way to *aliquo modo*.

586. ut...domo. This clause, which for emphasis is summed up and repeated in *id*, is the subject of *restat*.

me excutiam. Two interpretations are possible: (i) 'turn out my pockets,' (ii) 'decamp.' The latter is not supported by the balance of the sentence and makes *egrediar domo* a pleonasm.

587. nam ego...meus. Chremes is living entirely on his wife's money.

ACT IV, SCENE 2

Geta enters in a state of exultation. He does not at first see the old gentlemen.

591. hominem neminem. This emphatic pleonasm is found also in Cicero's letters.

592. quam Phormionem, sc. *vidi*. He might have said *quam Phormio*, sc. *est*. What he does say emphasizes the fact that he has actually seen Phormio's cleverness.

uenio: historic present with historic sequence.

593. argentum is the subject, *opus* the complement.

596. tempus sibi dari. The use of the accusative and infinitive with *gratias agere* is hardly found after Terence's time, *quod* with the indicative taking its place.

604. hinc unde, 'from the man from whom.' Both words are pronouns.

605. hospitem. Geta's little joke describes the man who has been some weeks or months away as a stranger.

ACT IV, SCENE 3

Antipho enters but is not seen by the others. His speeches are asides to himself.

606. exspecto...Geta, 'I am waiting to see how long it will be before Geta gets back.'

610. uolup seems to be the clipt neuter of an adjective *uolupis*, and here to be an adjective. It can also be used adverbially.

613. tun.... This is said to Demipho.

614. commodum, 'just now,' a colloquial use found in Cicero's letters.

625. auctores fuere = *suasere*.

ut praecipitem hanc daret, 'to turn the girl out neck and crop.'

629. ea eloquentiast. The words may be in the nominative or in the ablative, 'such is his eloquence' or 'of such eloquence is he.'

630. pono, 'I assume.'

631. capitis. If Phormio lost, then on his failure to pay the fine the loss of civic rights, ἀτιμία, *deminutio capitis*, would be decreed against him and he would become a slave to Demipho.

634. in manum. The phrase is used of underhand and corrupt transactions.

635. facessat, 'depart,' a quite classical meaning of the word where a command is made or implied.

636. satin...propitii? Madness was accounted a visitation of angry heaven.

638. ut est ille, ἅτε ὄντος ἐκείνου, 'he being, as he is.'

642. insanibat = *insaniebat*. The word was especially used of extravagance.

643. nimium quantum, *ἀμήχανον ὅσον*, 'ever so much,' a colloquial phrase but one that survived.

644. talentum magnum. The Attic talent is meant, other states having talents of less value.

645. adeo, 'precisely.'

647. non suscepisse. A new-born infant was laid on the threshold and unless the father acknowledged it by lifting it up it did not become legally his child. A rejected child was usually taken by someone, who reared it as a slave.

653. ad, 'as wife to.'

655. aliquantulum quae adferret, 'a wife to bring me a little bit.'

qui: abl. n.

661. animam debet. Such phrases as this and *ὀφείλειν τὴν ψυχήν* were natural in days when a debtor might be made a slave.

664. ne clama. This form of prohibition was supplanted in prose by the less brusque *noli clamare.*

668. sescentas, *μυρίας*, 'any number of.' Other words for any large number are *centum*, *trecenti*, *mille.*

674. quantum potest, 'as soon as possible,' the regular meaning of the phrase. Cf. 897.

675. mittam, 'dismiss.'

676. illi, i.e. the family of the invented lady.

679. adeo emphasizes *opportune.*

680. fructum, 'rents' if the farms were let, 'income' if they were managed by a bailiff. Cf. 789–790.

681. inde = *ab illo argento.*

ACT IV, SCENE 4

The old men go out and Antipho attacks Geta.

682. emunxi, *ἀπέμυξα*, 'I have wiped their noses,' i.e. have cheated them. The accusative is as after a verb of depriving.

683. satine est id? 'is that all?' The phrase is a sarcastic rebuke wilfully taken by Geta to refer to the amount of the money.

tantum iussus sum, sc. *emungere.*

686. restim. Since to the Greek hanging was of all forms of death the most degrading, to say that things were come to the rope was to express the depth of despair.

687. ut in this sense was supplanted by *utinam*.

688. exemplis. From this use of the word for a model or pattern punishment came the simple meaning of punishment, which it has in silver Latin.

689. mandes, 'you should entrust it.'

690. utibile is a colloquial word which soon became obsolete.

691. spes posse illam. The use of the accusative and infinitive with *spes* is found in all periods of Latin.

693. ducendast is more grim than *ducenda erit*.

694. noui is ironical, like *scilicet* in the next line.

699. iam, 'now then.'

701. tandem, 'at the worst.'

702. uocandi, sc. the guests.

705. postilla, i.e. since I became engaged.

709. brumam (*brevumam*) has its original meaning of the shortest day.

noui negoti incipere. There is no proof either that a partitive genitive can be used directly with a verb, as it is in Greek, or that *incipere* can be followed by a genitive. Perhaps Geta breaks off his sentence, substituting a gesture for the concluding words.

711. me uide, 'look to me,' i.e. 'trust me.'

ACT IV, SCENE 5

The old men return.

713. uerborum. The phrase *uerba dare*, to give words instead of deeds, regularly means to deceive or cheat.

duit, sc. Phormio.

714. hoc. He is carrying the money in a bag.

temere, lit. 'in the dark,' hence 'rashly.' Cf. l. 757.

715. Geta's remark is of course aside.

718. rem ipsam putasti, lit. 'you have calculated the exact sum,' i.e. 'you have exactly hit it.'

723. quid malum. The phrase is like the Elizabethan 'what the plague,' the adjective being the interjectional accusative. Our 'why the deuce' has the same construction. Cf. 948.

727. rogabo. Here Demipho and Geta exeunt.

illas, i.e. the Lemnian wife and daughter. Cf. l. 749.

ACT IV, SCENE 6

Sophrona enters in much distress. She does not see Chremes.

728. quo = *ad quem*.

732. a fratre meo, 'from my brother's house.' So παρ' ἡμῶν, 'from our house.' Cf. 840.

736. quid ago? The question in deliberative.

741. istorsum (*isto-versum*), 'this way.' He points. The use of *iste* in the sense of 'this' began in early Latin, became common in Imperial times, and was normal in medieval Latin. Here Chremes pulls Sophrona by the sleeve.

742. appellassis. This and the like subjunctive forms appear in Greek in forms like τιμήσω, used as futures no less than as subjunctives.

743. st. Though spelt without a vowel the word is a whole syllable.

745. eo, 'for this purpose.'

747. istoc is a causal ablative.

751. male factum. The words are a conventional expression of sorrow. In fact Chremes is relieved by the death of one who might get him into trouble with his Lemnian wife and whom he had long ago ceased to love.

754. duasne uxores habet? It is very natural but very comical that Chremes should forget that this was his own case. The passage is ruined if we accept the reading *duasne is uxores habet*, which further involves the elision of *au*. In the text *au* is shortened in hiatus.

ille quidem. This is a delightfully comic form of dramatic irony. Sophrona means by the words that Antipho is much too good and true a man to be false to her mistress, but to the audience the words reflect on Chremes who had supposed Antipho to be a bigamist and for the moment forgotten that he was one himself.

755. ergo like our exclamatory 'why' emphasizes an answer, especially an answer in one word.

759. ut uolebam, i.e. without its coming out that she is my daughter.

761. haec sola. Sophrona has distinctly said that the marriage was her doing. The reading *hic solus*, i.e. Antipho, though of higher authority, is hardly tolerable. As applied to Antipho the words *maxima sua cura* have no sound sense, for the translation '*by his great love*' seems impossible. Again it seems impossible that Chremes should here use *hic* of his nephew who is not on the stage and of whose whereabouts at the moment he knows nothing.

762. quid opus facto sit. The two simplest constructions with *opus* are seen in *quid opus est?* and *opus est facto*. Colloquially, as here, the two are combined, *quid* remaining the subject and *opus* the complement.

764. caue resciscat quisquam, 'take care no one gets to know it.'

765. scibit. This old Latin future was supplanted by the optative form *sciet*.

ACT V, SCENE I

After an interval Demipho and Geta return.

766. malis. The logical subject is *malos esse*, 'the being bad,' but the adjective is normally and naturally attracted to the case of the pronoun or substantive which follows the verb, in this instance *nobis* understood.

768. ita fugias.... The negative clause here is restrictive, and in restrictive clauses the negative is *ne*. The proverb commends running away but with the restriction that you do not overrun the place of safety. It is not known whether it refers to a runaway slave or to a game of hide-and-seek. Demipho means that he has shown excessive generosity.

quod aiunt, 'as the proverb goes.'

770. qui. A common form of the ablative which in time became an adverb.

771. recta praua faciunt. Here, as in Horace's *dicenda tacenda locutus*, the collocation of two opposite epithets means that the person spoken of makes no distinction between the qualities, does not care whether what he says is fit to be said or not, whether what he does is right or wrong.

772. illi is the adverb, =*in illa re*.

774. ut homost, 'seeing what a fellow he is.'

775. hem, mutet autem? 'what! change, do you say?'

776. ita faciam ut adducam, 'I will take the course of bringing,' is little more than a roundabout phrase for *adducam*.

777. prae is here an adverb according to its original use.

780. uorsura solues, 'you'll pay by borrowing,' and therefore be all the deeper in debt. Geta sees that in the end he must be found out, and then his punishment will be all the heavier for the shifts by which he has put it off.

781. in diem, 'for the present,' 'for the time being.'

783. huius. He points his thumb at Nausistrata who appears at the moment with Demipho.

ACT V, SCENE 2

786. re, 'your purse.'

787. factum uolo is sometimes a formula of gracious assent, as here, and sometimes an expression of content with one's past action.

789. talenta argenti bina. An income of £500 a year gave a position which would now require £2000 or more.

790. statim, 'regularly,' i.e. every yearly rent day or day of account with the bailiff. This sense of the word soon became obsolete.

capiebat. The lady characteristically thinks it needless to specify that she means her father, not her husband.

quid. This exclamatory use of *quis* and *quid*, although common in the comedians, is neglected by lexicographers, as is the like use of *qui* : cf. 911. Both words were afterwards supplanted by *quantum* and *quanto* and the like.

791. rebus uilioribus: abl. abs. The rise in prices ought to have raised the rents or the value of the produce.

792. quid haec uidentur ? sc. *tibi.*

scilicet. It is not a time for Demipho to defend or excuse his brother, so with a gesture he replies that it must be evident what he thinks of it.

794. possis, sc. *loqui.* Nausistrata, whatever her faults, does not set up to be younger than she is.

ACT V, SCENE 3

Chremes enters in some excitement and for the moment does not see his wife.

796. nollem. The potential mood implies that the money has been paid, as of course it has.

797. paene, sc. *dixeram*, the aoristic pluperfect. It is less natural to understand *dixi.*

798. iam recte. The answer is embarrassed and evasive. The verb is not definitely conceived.

804. hoc, causal ablative. 'That is why.' So often in Plautus.

806. perdis, 'you are ruining me,' is an agonized whisper to Demipho.

811. satis quaesitum, i.e. that I make no further inquiry.

814. in omnis, 'for all parties.'

819. Nausistrata being gone, Demipho turns with a natural testiness to ask for an explanation. As the audience know the facts, the dramatist finds a reason to send the old men indoors.

ACT V, SCENE 4

After a brief interval Antipho enters alone.

820. ut se habent might perhaps represent ἅτε οὕτως ἐχόντων, in which case Antipho declares his pleasure that one of the cousins has obtained his desire, even though it be Phaedria and not himself. It is however more likely that *ut* stands for *utut*, as occasionally in Cicero's letters.

822. quas. Classical Latin seems to supply no other instance of an accusative after *medeor*. We should perhaps read *quis*, a dative.

823. simul. We may translate this word by 'as soon as,' but the literal meaning is 'at one moment,' and a second *simul* is understood with *cura sese expediuit*. The use remained classical but perhaps *simul atque* (*ac*) was more common in this sense.

825. patefit. This is the colloquial use of the present for the future. The indicative implies his certainty that the facts will out.

ACT V, SCENE 5

Phormio enters and speaks without at first seeing Antipho.

830. propria poteretur, 'get the girl for his wife.'

emissast manu. The phrase was afterwards generally but not always crystallized into *manumissast*. A slave could not be wife to an Athenian.

835. ut fugitet, 'of skulking from.' This explanatory use of *ut* is common after nouns and pronouns.

837. Sunium. There seems to have been a slave-market at this town, which was at the southern point of Attica, now called Capo Colonna.

840. ostium concrepuit. This and other like passages have been much disputed. The best explanation seems to be as follows. It was not lawful at Athens to have a door opening directly on the street. The door was therefore set back at the end of a passage. A person who opens the door is heard to do so but is not seen until he emerges from the passage. The door creaks because it has no hinges but is constructed with sockets and pivots (*cardines*) which are of wood and do not fit very well. This explanation seems to get over all the difficulties.

ACT V, SCENE 6

Geta enters but does not see the others.

843. amicos. See note on 35. Geta would hardly speak so to his master's face.

844. pallio. The heavy Greek cloak was a hindrance to running but the difficulty was lessened if it was thrown round the neck. Slaves often ran in the streets of Athens, but gentlemen only under great necessity.

845. ut haec, quae contigerint, sciant. The confusion between a relative clause with the indicative and a dependent question with the subjunctive is common and natural enough. Livy often has it. Cf. 876.

847. em tibi, 'there you are!'

849. odio, 'annoying ways.' The adjective *odiosus* normally means distasteful or annoying. Cf. 937. The adjective of *odium* in the sense of hatred is *inuisus*.

853. quantum est qui uiuont...hominum, 'of all living men.' Like phrases are *quicquid est deum* and *quantum est hominum optimorum.*

858. tu quoque aderas. When a thing has been true for some time but not recognized, then on the recognition the imperfect may be used, like the Greek ἦν ἄρα. Cf. 945.

860. interea, not 'meanwhile' but, as usually in Virgil, 'after a time,' 'presently.' Cf. 91, 878.

867. suspenso gradu, ἐπ' ἄκροις τοῖς ποσίν, 'on tiptoe.'

871. mirificissumum. This superlative soon became obsolete and no other took its place.

872. Phanio. The dative of possession emphasizes the possession rather than the possessor. So here the emphasis is on the fatherhood. Compare Shakespeare's 'son to Polonius' and the like.

882. fecero. From the sense of 'you will find that I shall do it' the tense gets the sense of 'I shall do it at once.' The same change is seen in πεπράξεται and the like.

883. bene factum, 'I am deeply obliged to you.' The punctuation and distribution of the words here is doubtful. Although Antipho has already said *uale*, it seems best to assign these words to him and give them their usual sense. Antipho may say them as he goes out and rather of than to Phormio.

ACT V, SCENE 7

Phormio is alone.

884. datam, sc. *esse*.

886. adimere = *adimendi*.

889. hoc qui cogam, sc. *senes*, 'the means to enforce this on the old gentlemen.' The accusative of the inner object is common with *cogo*.

ACT V, SCENE 8

Phormio is hiding in the alley when the old men enter.

902. It is usual to scan *uerĕbamini*. It may be suggested that here *u'rēbamini* and in Hec. 202 *u'rīs esse* are more likely scansions. In English we have dropt the initial letter in such words as 'wrought' but once it presented no difficulty, because the *r* was rolled as in Latin. Cf. 787.

904. quantaquanta. Of these duplicated forms *quisquis* survived, but *utut* and the others were supplanted by words with the suffix *-cumque*.

911. qui is exclamatory, = *οἷος*.

917. contempserim. The subjunctive is causal as in 960 and in Dido's *quos ego sim toties iam dedignata*, 'how can I go to them when I have spurned them again and again?'

922. rescribi, 'to be re-transferred' at the banker's from Phormio's account to Demipho's.

923. quodne ego.... The sentence is elliptical, the full construction being *iubeamne rescribi id quod ego* etc.

926. hic. He slaps his pocket.

928. alterae. This form of the dative feminine occurs occasionally in later writers, e.g. Nepos. For using it Boswell once had to defend himself against Johnson.

930. in' = *isne*, 'won't you go,' i.e. 'go.'

931. fugitiue. The sense is merely abusive, as with the like use of *fur*.

932. adeo, 'to boot.'

933. ut...habitet depends on *duces* or *uis ducere* understood.

935. quaeso, quid narras? Phormio professes not to take Demipho's meaning.

945. ut ludos facit, sc. *nobis*, 'how he makes game of us!'

947. argentum...condonamus te. The accusative of the person with *condono* is found only in the comedians.

949. inconstantia. This is Fleckeisen's correction of *sententia*, which gives an intolerable rhythm. Perhaps the corrupt word is not *sententia* but *puerili*, which may be a gloss for some rarer word. [Cf. Hec. 312.]

954. monstri. Weak men like Chremes fly to supernatural explanations.

957. praesenti. Cf. our 'keep your wits about you' and 'presence of mind.'

960. Chreme: an heteroclitic vocative.

964. gladiatorio. Perhaps the word in the original was ληστικῷ. Terence may have forgotten that there were no gladiators at Athens, or he may use the name by transference for a swashbuckler.

966. hoc...quom, 'this fact that.' In this sense *quom* was supplanted by *quod*, both words being neuter accusatives of the relative pronoun.

967. e medio excessit. Many languages show an unwillingness to speak directly of death.

970. ain tu? 'what do you mean?'

971. sis ueritus feminae. The genitive is as after *fastidio*, *miseret* and the like. The use with *uereor* is colloquial and is found in Cicero's letters.

974. dabo, θήσω, *faciam*.

978. publicitus. The word soon became obsolete, *publice* supplanting it. The old word for the Treasury was *publicum* and the suffix *-itus* means 'from.'

981. huc. He points to Chremes' house where Nausistrata is.

983. The two old men struggle to hold Phormio.

iniuria = *actio iniuriae*.

989. est ubi, 'there is one with whom.' The reference of course is to Nausistrata, and *ubi* is a pronoun.

ACT V, SCENE 9

In the midst of the struggle Nausistrata comes out of the house. Phormio shakes himself free from the old men and Chremes cowers away. Tableau.

990. qui = *quis*.

993. creduis. The MSS. give *credas* against the metre. The correct form *creduis* seems more probable in Terence than the incorrectly formed *creduas*, which was also in use.

1004. clam te. As after *clanculum* the case after *clam* is the accusative. As a preposition the word died out.

1005. mi homo, 'my good man.' The phrase is usual in angry protest, especially to one of inferior rank, as here to Phormio.

1009. hoc actumst. Chremes had asked his brother what could be done: Phormio says scornfully that in this case nothing can be done because all the doing is over. A like use of the perfect is seen in *uixerunt*, 'they are dead,' *fuit*, 'it is no more,' *actum est*, 'all's up.'

hodie, as in 377.

1012. haecine for *haecene*, *haece* being fem. pl. and when used alone shortened to *haec*, a form which survived in poetry.

1015. sed ea quin sit ignoscenda.... He finishes the sentence with a gesture which implies *uix negabis*. The sentence can hardly be taken as a question because questions with *quin* are questions only in form while in sense they are usually imperatives or statements akin to imperatives. Moreover there would be a difficulty in the mood of *sit*. See on 209.

uerba fiunt mortuo. The meaning is not known for certain. (i) You talk to the dead, i.e. to one who cannot hear. Then the reference is to Nausistrata who is no more willing to have excuses for Chremes than the dead are able. (ii) You speak a funeral oration, i.e. one in which a man's virtues are exaggerated and his faults made little of. Then Phormio means that Demipho is trying to make the best of a poor case. We may compare the American funeral sermon, 'Let us remember his virtues, if he had any, and forget his vices, if we can.'

1018. compressit, 'seduced.'

1019. qui. As regularly the pronoun is attracted into the gender of the complement.

1020. alia, τὰ ἄλλα, 'all other.' The use of *alii* for *ceteri*, generally colloquial, is found once in Horace: *obstrictis aliis praeter Iapyga.*

1021. quid ego, sc. *feram.*

defungier is probably impersonal as in Ad. 507 *utinam hic sit modo defunctum,* 'I only wish there were an end to it here.'

1026. Phormio uses the crier's phrase to announce a funeral.

exsequias. Like *domum* etc. this accusative retained its original use without a preposition.

1027. dabo: colloquial for *faciam* and more vigorous. From the root DA come δίδωμι and *do,* from the root DHA τίθημι and *facio*; but, since in Latin *dh* in the middle of a word became not *f,* but *d,* in early compounds both roots gave the same form. This perhaps accounts for that use of *do* for *facio* which is so common in early Latin.

1031. credo is ironical, as often. The phrase seems to be addrest to her husband and instead of finishing it she turns and addresses Demipho.

1033. minime gentium, 'not the least in the world.' The phrase is a strong colloquial negative.

1034. non potest. The subject is *quod factumst* understood.

1035. purgat. This intransitive use in the sense of 'apologizes' is very uncommon.

1040. Nausistrata rounds fiercely on her husband who collapses.

1042. ore. So we say 'how can you have the face to do it?'

1048. et praeter spem. These words he adds aside.

1052. quod here, as in the next line, is the accusative of the inner object.

1055. Ω. It is not known whether this symbol represented the last actor to speak, in this play Phormio, or is, as Bentley thought, a corruption of CA standing for *cantor.* In some cases the *cantica* or songs of the play were sung by a professional musician while the actor made the appropriate gestures.

VOCABULARY

Except where so-called rules are given in the grammars, as for final syllables and some others, long vowels, as far as the length can be ascertained, are marked throughout. It is probable that before *f* and *s* the letter *n* was not pronounced as a consonant but nasalized and lengthened the preceding vowel. This is almost certain in the case of the vowels *i* and *o*, perhaps hardly less certain in the case of *a*, *e* and *u*. In the case of some words the 'hidden quantity,' as it is called, is not certainly known. Of course the quantity of the scanning unit is known but that does not tell the quantity of the vowel. Thus *actos* and *factos* are each a spondee, but in the one *a* is long, in the other short.

ABBREVIATIONS

1, 2, 3, 4	the conjugations	*impers.*	impersonal
m. f. n.	the genders	*interj.*	interjection
c.	masculine or feminine	*interrog.*	interrogative
abl.	ablative	*irreg.*	irregular
adv.	adverb	*prep.*	preposition
conj.	conjunction	*pron.*	pronoun
def.	defective	*rel.*	relative
dep.	deponent	*v. a.*	verb active (transitive)
gen.	genitive	*v. n.*	verb neuter (intransitive)

Terence uses some forms which ceased to be normal soon after his time. In the present play the following may be noticed.

A fourth declension genitive of the form of *metuis*. This follows the analogy of *u*-stems of the third declension.

In the genitive and dative of *qui*, *quis*, and their compounds the forms used are *quoius* and *quoi*.

With *hic* there is a tendency to keep *-ce* throughout, as in *hōrunce*, *hīsce* (n. pl. and dat. and abl.). On the other hand *eccum* is for *ecce hum*.

A by-form of *ipse* is *ipsus*.

In the present subjunctive of *sum* and its compounds we have *siem*, *sies*, *siet*, *sient*. These original optative forms gave way to *sim*, etc., oddly formed to fit *simus* and *sitis*.

Aorist subjunctives of the form of *appellāssis*, *faxo*, *faxit*. Like other subjunctives these could be used as futures.

The original imperative forms *dīce*, *dūce*, *face*. These were already giving way to the clipt forms, *dic*, etc.

Fourth conjugation futures and imperfects of the form of *scībit*, *insanībat*.

Present infinitives middle and passive of the form of *mīrārier*, *adipīscier*, *experīrier*.

Gerunds and gerundives of the form of *dīcundi*, *incipiundus*.

In the present subjunctive of *do* and its compounds there are the forms *duim*, *duis*, *duit*, *duint*. In the compounds there may also have been strange forms of the type of *creduam*, *creduant*. It should be noted that the verb *do* does not belong to the first conjugation though a few of its forms were assimilated to the forms of that conjugation. Such are *das*, *dat*, *dant*, *da*, *dandi*.

Some shortened forms which probably remained current in conversation. Such are *dīxti*, *intrīsti*, *intellexti*, *īn* for *īsne*, *sānum* for *sānusne*.

a, **ab**, **abs**, prep. *from*, *by* (of the agent), *in* (340 note).

ab-dūco, -dūxi, -ductum, v. a. 3 *lead off*.

ab-eo, -ii, -itum, -īre, v. n. irreg. *go off*, *go away*; **abi**, *go along with you*.

abhinc, adv. *ago*.

ab-rādo, -rāsi, -rāsum, v. a. 3 *scrape off*.

ab-ripio, -ripui, -reptum, v. a. 3 *snatch away*.

absque, prep. + conj. *if without*.

ab-sum, āfui, abesse, v. n. *am away*, *am absent*.

ab-sūmo, -sūmpsi, -sūmptum, v. a. 3 *take away*.

ab-undo, v. n. 1 *overflow*.

ab-utor, -ūsus sum, v. dep. 3 *misuse*.

ac, conj. *and*, *and moreover*, *as*.

ac-cēdo, -cessi, -cessum, v. n. 3 *am added*.

ac-cido, -cidi, v. n. 3 *befall*.

ac-cingo, -cinxi, -cīnctum, v. a. 3 *gird up*; **accingor**, *gird up my loins*, *prepare myself*.

ac-cipio, -cēpi, -ceptum, v. a. 3 *receive*, *accept*.

accipiter, -tris, m. *hawk* (Pliny speaks of sixteen species).

ac-curro, -cucurri, -cursum, v. n. 3 *run up*.

ac-cūso, v. a. 1 *accuse*.

ācer, -cris, -cre, *sharp*, *severe*.

āctor, -ōris, m. *stage-manager*, *player*.

āctūtum, adv. *at once* (āctu + tum).

ad, prep. *to*.

ad-do, -didi, -ditum, -dere, v. a. irreg. *add*.

ad-dūco, -dūxi, -ductum, v. a. 3 *bring here, bring up.*
ad-eo, -ii, -itum, -īre, v. n. irreg. *go up, apply.*
adeo, adv. *to this point, so much, so, precisely, very, moreover:* (sometimes merely emphasizes the preceding word).
ad-fecto, v. a. 1 *take* (a road or way).
ad-fero, -tuli, -lātum, -ferre, v. a. irreg. *bring, bring here.*
ad-ficio, -fēci, -fectum, v. a. 3 *furnish with, trouble.*
adfinis, -e, *connected by marriage, connexion by marriage.*
ad-gnōsco, -gnōui, -gnitum, v. a. 3 *recognize.*
ad-gredior, -gressus sum, v. dep. 3 *attack.*
ad-hibeo, v. a. 2 *call in, send for.*
adhuc, adv. *up to now, still.*
ad-imo, -ēmi, -emptum, v. a. 3 *take away.*
ad-ipiscor, -eptus sum, v. dep. 3 *get, obtain.*
adiūmentum, -i, n. *help.*
adiūto, v. a. 1 *help.*
adiūtor, -ōris, m. *helper.*
ad-loquor, -locūtus sum, v. dep. 3 *speak to.*
ad-mitto, -mīsi, -missum, v. a. 3 *commit* (a fault).
admodum, adv. *very, very much so, just so, yes certainly.*
ad-moueo, -mōui, -mōtum, v. a. 2 *move up, bring near.*
ad-orior, -ortus sum, -orīri, v. dep. 3 and 4 *attack.*
ad-porto, v. a. 1 *bring here, carry here, carry up.*
ad-probo, v. a. 1 *approve.*
ad-sequor, -secūtus sum, v. dep. 3 *follow close.*
ad-simulo, v. n. 1 *pretend, assume an air.*
ad-sto, -stiti, v. n. 1 *stand near.*
ad-sum, -fui, -esse, v. n. *am here, assist.*
ad-uenio, -uēni, -uentum, v. n. 4 *arrive.*
aduentus, -i and -us, m. *arrival.*
aduersārius, -i, m. *opponent.*
ad-uerto, -uerti, -uersum, v. a. 3 *turn to;* **animum aduerto**, *notice, observe.*
ad-uigilo, v. n. 1 *keep awake.*
adulēscens, -ntis, m. *lad, young man:* adj. *young.*
adulēscentia, -ae, f. *youthfulness, youthful age.*
ad-uoco, v. a. 1 *summon, summon to aid me.*
ad-uorsor, v. dep. 1 *am opposed.*
aduorsum, prep. *against.*
aduorsus, -a, -um, *meeting, unpropitious.*
aedes, -ium, f. *house.*
aediculae, -ārum, f. *little house, cottage.*
aegre, adv. *sickly;* **aegre est mihi**, *I fret.*
aegritūdo, -inis, f. *sickness, illness.*
aequālis, -e, *of one's own age, friend.*
aequanimitas, -ātis, f. *fairness of mind.*
aeque, adv. *equally, as much.*
aequos, -a, -om, *fair, right.*
aerumna, -ae, f. *trouble.*
aetas, -ātis, f. *age, life.*
age, interj. *come now! come!*
ager, -ri, m. *land, farm.*

agito, v. a. 1 *stir up*.
ago, ēgi, āctum, v. a. 3 *deal with, arrange, plead* (a cause), *play* (a part), *bring* (an action at law); **hoc ago**, *am attentive*.
ah, interj. *ah! dear me!* (*baugh!*).
ain = aisne.
aio, v. defective, *say, say yes*.
alicunde, pron. and adv. *from someone, from somewhere*.
aliēnus, -a, -um, *another's, strange*.
aliqua, adv. *somehow*.
aliquantulum, adv. used as noun, *a trifle*.
aliquis, -qua, -quid, indef. pron. *some, someone*.
aliquot, pronominal adj. *several*.
aliter, adv. *otherwise*.
alius, -a, -ud, *other, the other* (see 1020 note).
alo, alui, altum, v. a. 3 *feed, support*.
alter, -era, -erum, *second, other*.
ambo, -ae, -o, *both, the pair* (dual number).
ambulo, v. a. 1 *walk*.
amīca, -ae, f. *friend, mistress*.
amīcitia, -ae, f. *friendship*.
amīcus, -i, m. *friend*.
ā-mitto, -mīsi, -missum, v. a. 3 *send away, let go, let off, part with, lose*.
amo, v. a. 1 *love*; **amo te**, *I thank you*.
amor, -ōris, m. *love*.
ā-moueo, -mōui, -mōtum, v. a. 2 *move off*.
amplius, adv. comparative, *longer, further, to a larger extent*.
an, interrogative particle direct and indirect, *if, whether, or*.
ancilla, -ae, f. *servant girl*.
angiportum, -i, n. and **angiportus**, -i or -us, m. *alley*.
ango, anxi, v. a. 3 *throttle, torture*.
anguis, -is, m. *snake*.
anicula, -ae, f. *poor old woman*.
anima, -ae, f. *breath*.
animaduerto, animum aduerto: see **aduerto**.
animus, -i, m. *mind*.
ante, prep. and adv. *before*.
ante-cēdo, -cessi, -cessum, v. n. 3 *arrive earlier*.
ante-pōno, -posui, -positum, v. a. 3 *prefer*.
antīquos, -a, -om, *old, of long standing*.
anus, -us, f. *old woman*.
aperte, adv. *openly*.
apīscor, aptus sum, v. dep. 3 *get, obtain*.
ap-paro, v. a. 1 *prepare*.
appello, v. a. 1 *call, appeal to*.
ap-pōno, -posui, -positum, v. a. 3 *put on the table*.
apud, prep. *with, near, in the house of, in the hands of*.
arbitror, v. dep. 1 *think*.
argentarius, -a, -um, *concerning money*.
argentum, -i, n. *cash*.
ars, artis, f. *skill, art*.
artifex, -icis, c. *craftsman*.
as-porto, v. a. 1 *carry off, transport*.
astūte, adv. *cunningly*.
asymbolus, *not contributing* (ἀσύμβολος = immūnis).
at, conj. *but, why now, it may be said*.
atauos, -i, m. *great-grandfather's grandfather*.

āter, -ra, -rum, *coal-black.*
atque, conj. *and, and moreover, as.*
atqui, conj. *but for all that.*
attat, interj. *bother it! hang it!*
attendo, -tendi, -tentum, v. a. 3 *stretch, apply.*
at-tineo, -tinui, -tentum, v. n. 2 *belong, concern.*
at-tingo, -tigi, -tāctum, v. a. 3 *touch.*
au, interj. used by women, *oh! oh dear no! don't!*
auāritia, -ae, f. *greed.*
auctor, -ōris, m. *adviser.*
audācia, -ae, f. *venturesomeness, audacity.*
audācissime: superlative of **audācter**.
audācter, adv. *boldly, audaciously.*
audāx, gen. -ācis, *venturous, daring, bold, impudent.*
audeo, ausus sum, audere, v. n. 2 *am eager for, dare.*
audio, v. a. 4 *hear, am spoken of, am told* (see 160 note).
au-fero, abstuli, ablātum, auferre, v. a. irreg. *carry off.* (**au** is an old preposition which survives only in a few compounds, where it is used in the sense of **ab**.)
auos, -i, m. *grandfather.*
auris, -is, f. *ear.*
aurum, -i, n. *gold.*
ausculto, v. a. and n. 1 *listen to, listen.*
aut, conj. *either, or, or else.*
autem, conj. (= δέ) *now, well, but.* (Also used in questions which express surprise.)
auxilium, -li, n. *help.*

balineae, -ārum, f. *baths.*
beātus, -a, -um, *blest, happy.*
bēlua, -ae, f. (large beast), *fool, dolt.*
bene, adv. *well.*
benedictum, -i, n. *kind word.*
benigne, adv. *kindly.*
benignus, -a, -um, *kind.*
beniuolus, -a, -um, *well-wishing.*
bīni, -ae, -a, *two each, two.*
blande, adv. *winsomely, coaxingly.*
bonitas, -ātis, f. *goodness.*
bona, -ōrum, n. *goods, property.*
bonus, -a, -um, *good, useful.*
brūma, -ae, f. *shortest day.*

callidus, -a, -um, *skilful, cunning.*
calx, calcis, f. *heel.*
canis, -is, c. *hound, dog.*
cano, cecini, cantātum, v. n. 3 *sing.*
cantilēna, -ae, f. *old song, silly old song.*
capillus, -i, m. *hair.*
capio, cēpi, captum, v. a. 3 *take, seize, receive.*
capto, v. a. 1 *catch at, try to catch.*
caput, -itis, n. *head, person, life, civic status.*
carcer, -eris, m. *jail, jail-bird.*
casa, -ae, f. *hut, cottage.*
caueo, cāui, cautum, v. a. and n. 3 *beware, beware of;* **caue** with subj. 2nd pers. a. *do not.*
causa, -ae, f. *cause, pretext, sake.*
cautus, -a, -um, *cautious.*
cedo, imperative of **do** with adverbial prefix: *give me, bring me, tell me.*

celere, adv. *quickly* (supplanted by **celeriter**).
cēlo, v. a. 1 *hide*.
cēna, -ae, f. dinner. (The usual hour for it was about sundown.)
cēnseo, cēnsui, cēnsum, v. a. 2 *vote, think best*.
certe, adv. *surely*.
certo, adv. *certainly, for sure*.
certus, -a, -um, *decided, resolved, sure*; **certior**, *informed*.
cerua, -ae, f. *hind*. (The species was the Red Deer.)
cesso, v. n. 1 *am slow, hesitate, make a pause*.
cēteri, -ae, -a, *the other, the rest, the others*.
cēterum, conj. *be that as it may, however*.
circum-eo, -ii, -itum, -īre, v. a. irreg. *cheat*.
citharistria, -ae, f. *cittern-player*.
ciuis, -is, c. *free member of the state*. (Not a slave or foreigner.)
clam, prep. *unknown to*. [N.B. used with the accusative, not with the ablative.]
clāmo, v. n. 1 *cry out*.
clanculum, adv. *secretly*.
coepi, v. preteritive, 3 *begin*.
coepto, v. a. 1 *attempt*.
cōgito, v. a. 1 *think*.
cōgnātus, -a, -um, *akin*.
cō-gnōsco, -gnōui, -gnitum, v. a. 3 *recognize*.
cōgo (cum + ago), coēgi, coāctum, v. a. 3 *coerce, compel*.
coitio, -ōnis, f. *encounter*.
colo, colui, cultum, v. a. 3 *till, cultivate*.
columen, -inis, n. *pillar, prop*.
cōmiter, adv. *obligingly*.
com-memini, v. preteritive, 3 *remember well*.
com-memoro, v. a. 1 *relate, state formally*.
com-mendo, v. a. 1 *entrust*.
com-mereo, v. a. 2 *deserve*.
comminīscor, commentus sum, v. dep. 3 *devise*.
commodus, -a, -um, *fitting, profitable*.
com-moror, v. dep. 1 *stay*.
com-moueo, -mōui, -mōtum, v. a. 2 *stir, affect, upset*.
commūnis, -e, *shared by many*.
com-mūto, v. a. 1 *exchange*.
cōmoedia, -ae, f. *comedy*.
com-paro, v. a. 1 *arrange*.
com-perio, -peri, -pertum, v. a. 4 *ascertain*.
compes, -edis, f. *fetter*.
complūres, -ia (later -a), *several, a good many*.
composito, adv. *by arrangement, on purpose*.
com-primo, -pressi, -pressum, v. a. 3 *suppress, seduce, hold* (one's breath).
con-cēdo, -cessi, -cessum, v. a. and n. 3 *grant, step aside*.
con-clūdo, -si, -sum, v. a. 3 *shut up, cage*.
concordo, v. n. 1 *am in agreement with*.
con-crepo, -crepui, -crepitum, v. n. 1 *creak*.
condicio, -ōnis, f. *match, marriage*.
con-dōno, v. a. 1 *make a present of, forgive* (a debt).
con-ficio, -fēci, -factum, v. a. 3 *make up, complete, run through*.
confīdens, -ntis, *impudent, brazen*.

con-fingo, -finxi, -fictum, v. a. 3 *make up, invent.*

con-fiteor, -fessus sum, v. dep. 2 *confess.*

conflicto, v. n. 1 *struggle, fight.*

confūto, v. a. 1 *stop from boiling over, repress.*

con-gredior, -gressus sum, v. dep. 3 *meet.*

congruo, congrui, v. n. 3 *agree.*

con-icio, -iēci, -iectum, v. a. 3 *compare.*

coniūnx, coniugis, c. *wife, husband.*

con-loco, v. a. 1 *match, settle in marriage.*

con-loquor, -locutus sum, v. dep. 3 *talk with.*

cōnor, v. dep. 1 *try.*

con-rādo, -si, -sum, v. a. 3 *scrape together.*

conscius, -a, -um, *jointly aware, having on the conscience.*

consilium, -li, n. *advice.*

conspectus, -us, m. *clear view.*

con-stituo, -stitui, -stitūtum, v. a. and n. 3 *arrange, agree.*

con-suēsco, -suēui, -suētum, v. n. 3 *associate, keep company.*

consuētūdo, -inis, f. *intercourse.*

consulo, -sului, -sultum, v. a. and n. 3 *devise, advise.*

con-temno, -tempsi, -temptum, v. a. 3 *slight.*

contemplor, v. dep. 1 *gaze, gaze at.*

con-tero, -trīui, -trītum, v. a. 3 *spend, waste.*

con-tineo, -tinui, -tentum, v. a. 2 *keep.*

con-tingo, -tigi, -tāctum, v. a. 3 *befall, befall as a good thing.*

continuo, adv. *at once.*

contortor, -ōris, m. *perverter* [a nonce word].

contra, adv. and prep. *on the other hand, against.*

contrōuersia, -ae, f. *dispute.*

contumēlia, -ae, f. *insult.*

contumēliōse, adv. *insultingly.*

conuāso, v. a. 1 *pack up.*

con-uenio, -uēni, -uentum, v. a. and n. 4 *agree, agree with, meet, interview.*

cōpia, -ae, f. *means, means of meeting, abundance.*

cor, cordis, n. *heart, mind;* **cordi**, locative case, *in the heart*, i.e. *dear.*

cōram, adv. *face to face.*

cottīdiānus, -a, -um, *daily.*

cras, adv. *to-morrow.*

crēber, -bra, -brum, *frequent.*

crēdo, -didi, -ditum, v. a. and n. 3 *believe, entrust;* **creduim**, pres. subjunctive.

crēsco, crēui, crētum, v. n. 3 *grow.*

crīmen, -inis, n. *reproach, accusation.*

crux, crucis, f. *cross, crucifixion* (especially in the quasi-compound **malam crucem** or **malamcrucem**).

culpa, -ae, f. *blame, fault.*

cum, prep. *with, because possest of.*

cupiditas, -ātis, f. *desire.*

cupidus, -a, -um, *eager.*

cupio, -iui and -ii, -itum, v. a. 3 *am eager for.*

cūra, -ae, f. *anxiety, trouble.*

cūro, v. a. 1 *see to.*

curro, cucurri, cursum, v. n. 3 *run.*

cursus, -us, m. *run, running.*

custos, -ōdis, m. *guardian.*

damno, v. a. 1 *find guilty*, *give a verdict against.*
damnum, -i, n. *loss.*
de, prep. *from*, *down from*, *concerning*, *in accordance with.*
dea, -ae, f. *goddess.*
dēbeo (de + habeo), v. a. 2 *owe.*
dē-cipio, -cēpi, -ceptum, v. a. 3 *deceive.*
de-cumbo, -cubui, v. n. 3 *lie down*, *take a place at the dinner table.*
dē-fendo, -fendi, -fensum, v. a. 3 *ward off*, *defend.*
dē-fero, -tuli, -lātum, -ferre, v. a. irreg. *carry.*
dē-fetīscor, -fessus, v. dep. 3 *grow very weary.*
dē-ficio, -fēci, -fectum, v. n. 3 *fall short*, *fail.*
dē-fit, v. defective, *am lacking.* [Forms found are dēfit, defīat, dēfīet, dēfīeri.]
dē-frūdo (fraudo), v. a. 1 *cheat.*
dē-fungor, -fūnctus sum, v. dep. 3 *have done with.*
dē-go (de + ago), v. a. 3 *pass* (time), *live.*
dē-hortor, v. dep. 1 *dissuade.*
dē-lībero, v. a. 1 *weigh*, *consider maturely.*
dē-libūtus, -a, -um, *smeared over* (metaphorically).
dēlīro, v. n. 1 *am mad*, *rave.*
dēmensum, -i, n. *allowance.*
dē-mīror, v. dep. 1 *greatly wonder.*
dē-monstro, v. a. 1 *show.*
dē-narro, v. a. 1 *tell in full*, *tell in detail.*
dēnique, adv. *at last*, *in fine.*
dēnuo (de + nouo), adv. *anew.*
dē-pecīscor, -pāctus sum, v. dep. 3 *make a bargain.*
dē-pingo, -pinxi, -pīctus, v. n. 3 *portray.*
dē-prāuo, v. a. 1 *make worse*, *pervert.*
dē-puto, v. a. 1 *reckon.*
dē-rīuo, v. a. 1 *bring down a stream* (from a reservoir).
dē-sino, -sii, -situm, v. n. 3 *cease.*
dē-sisto, -stiti, v. n. 3 *cease.*
dē-spondeo, -spondi, -sponsum, v. a. 2 *pledge*, *betroth.*
dē-sum, -fui, -esse, v. n. *am lacking*, *fail.*
dē-uerbero, v. a. 1 *whip hard.*
dē-uīto, v. a. 1 *shun.*
dē-uortor, -uorsus sum, v. dep. (middle) 3 *turn aside.*
deus, -i, m. *god.*
dica, -ae, f. *lawsuit*, *action.*
dico, v. a. 1 *set apart.*
dīco, dixi, dīctum, v. a. 3 *say*, *plead* (a cause).
dīctio, -ōnis, f. *saying*, *giving* (of evidence).
dīctito, v. a. 1 *say often*, *say emphatically.*
dies, -ēi and -e, c. (m. in pl.) *day*, *present moment.*
dīgnus, -a, -um, *fit*, *worthy.*
dī-gredior, -gressus, v. dep. 3 *go apart.*
dī-lapido, v. a. 1 *make ducks and drakes of.*
dīmidius, -a, -um, *half.*
dis, gen. dītis, *rich.*
dis-cēdo, -cessi, -cessum, v. n. 3 *go away*, *get off.*
dīsco, didici, v. a. 3 *learn.*
di-scrībo, -scrīpsi, -scrīptum, v. a. 3 *pay to several persons.*

dis-simulo, v. a. 1 *conceal.*
dis-soluo, -solui, -solūtum, v. a. 3 *pay off.*
dis-taedet, v. impersonal, 2 *is very distasteful, is wearying.*
dis-traho, -trāxi, -trăctum, v. a. 3 *drag apart.*
diu, adv. *for a long time, long.*
diūtinus, -a, -um, *long.*
do, dedi, datum, dare, v. irreg. *give, grant, make, say, deal with, give in marriage.*
doleo, v. n. 2 *feel pain;* **dolet**, impersonal, *it pains.*
dominus, -i, m. *owner.*
domus, -us, f. *house, home;* **domi** (locative), *at home, in one's possession.*
dōnec, conj. *until.*
dormio, v. n. 4 *sleep.*
dos, dōtis, f. *dowry.*
dōtāta, *dowered, a wife with a dowry.*
dubito, v. a. 1 *doubt.*
dūco, dūxi, dŭctum, v. a. 3 *lead, lead astray, marry.*
dūcto, v. a. 1 *elope with.*
dūdum, adv. *for some time past, some time ago, before.*
duim, duis, etc., present subjunctive of **do**.
-dum, an emphasizing enclitic used with imperatives and interjections.
dum, conj. *while, until, provided that, because.*
duo, -ae, -o, dual numeral, *two.*
duplex, gen. -icis, *double.*
dūrus, -a, -um, *hard, difficult.*

e, **ex**, prep. *out of, from, in accordance with.*
ecastor, interj. (used by women) *on my word.*
ecce, interj. *see!*
eccerē, interj. *there now! see there!*
eccum (ecce + hum) interj. + pron.: *see him, here he is.*
ecquis, -que, -quid, indef. interrog. pron. *is there any?*
edāx, gen. -ācis, *gormandizing.*
edepol, interj. *on my word.*
ē-doceo, -docui, -doctum, v. a. 2 *teach thoroughly.*
ef-fero, extuli, ēlātum, efferre, v. a. irreg. *carry out, publish.*
ef-ficio, -fēci, -fectum, v. a. 3 *accomplish.*
ef-fūttio, v. a. 4 *allow to leak out, blab.*
egeo, v. n. 2 *am in extreme poverty.*
egestas, -ātis, f. *extreme poverty.*
ego, pers. pron. *I.*
egomet, emphasized form of **ego**.
ē-gredior, -gressus sum, v. dep. 3 *go out.*
ēgregius, -a, -um, *beyond the common, notable.*
ehem, interj. *bless me! I say!*
eho, interj. *bless me! good heavens!*
ei, interj. *dear me!* **ei mihi**, *hang it all!*
ē-icio, -iēci, -iectum, v. a. 3 *evict, turn out.*
ēloquentia, -ae, f. *eloquence.*
ē-loquor, -locutus sum, v. dep. 3 *speak out.*
ē-lūdo, -lūsi, -lūsum, v. a. 3 *cheat.*
em, interj. *take it, there you are.*
ē-mitto, -mīsi, -missum, v. a. 3 *send out;* **emitto manu**, *liberate, make free.*

emo, ēmi, emptum, v. a. 3 *buy.*

ē-morior, -mortuus sum, -mori and -moriri (archaic), v. dep. 3 *die at once.*

ē-mungo, -munxi, -munctum, v. a. 3 (wipe the nose) *chouse.*

en, interj. *see! look!*

ē-nico, -nicui, -nectum and -necātum, v. a. 1 *kill, plague to death.*

enim, adv. *indeed.*

enimuēro, adv. *of a truth.*

ē-nītor, -nīsus and -nīxus sum, v. dep. 3 *work hard.*

ēnumquam, emphatic interrogative form of **umquam**.

eo, adv. *to that place, to that point, to such an extent.*

eo, ii, itum, īre, v. n. irreg. *go.*

epistula, -ae, f. *letter.*

equidem, adv. *indeed* (emphasizing prefix + quidem).

era, -ae, f. *lady of the house, mistress.*

ergo, adv. *therefore, why there, why, that is why, then* (in questions).

erīlis, -e, *of a master or mistress.*

ē-ripio, -ripui, -reptum, v. a. 3 *rescue.*

erro, v. n. 1 *wander, make a mistake.*

ē-rumpo, -rūpi, -ruptum, v. n. 3 *break out, end in.*

erus, -i, m. *master of the house, master.*

est ut, *it is the fact that.*

et, conj. *and.*

etiam, adv. *also, even, as well, indeed, at all, still, as yet, yes.*

etsi, conj. *although.*

eu, interj. *bravo!*

e-uādo, -uāsi, -uāsum, v. n. 3 *go to a point.*

ē-uenio, -uēni, -uentum, v. n. 4 *happen.*

ē-uoluo, -uolui, -uolutum, v. a. 3 *extricate.*

ex: see **e.**

exaduorsum, adv. *opposite.*

ex-animo, v. a. 1 *deprive of breath* or *of presence of mind.*

ex-cēdo, -cessi, -cessum, v. n. 3 *go out.*

ex-cerpo, -cerpsi, -cerptum, v. a. 3 *strike out, omit.*

ex-clāmo, v. n. 1 *cry out.*

ex-crucio, v. a. 1 *torture severely.*

ex-cutio, -cussi, -cussum, v. a. 3 *shake out.*

ex-edo, -ēdi, -essum (later ēsum), -esse, v. a. irreg. *eat up.*

exemplum, -i, n. *pattern, model, fashion, form of punishment.*

ex-eo, -ii, -itum, -ire, v. n. irreg. *go out.*

ex-īstumo, v. a. 1 *reckon, think.*

ex-onero, v. a. 1 *relieve of a burden.*

ex-ōro, v. a. 1 *induce by entreaty, gain by entreaty.*

ex-pedio, v. a. 4 *disentangle, explain.*

expedit, *it is profitable.*

ex-perior, -pertus sum, v. dep. 4 *try.*

ex-peto, -petii, -petītum, v. a. 3 *try hard to get.*

expiscor, v. dep. 1 *try to fish out.*

ex-plōro, v. a. 1 *think out, track out.*

ex-sculpo, -sculpsi, -sculptum, v. a. 3 *dig out, knock out.*

exsequiae, -ārum, f. *funeral, funeral service.*
exsilium, -li, n. *exile.*
ex-specto, v. a. 1 *look for, wait for, wait to see.*
ex-stillo, v. n. 1 *trickle away.*
ex-timēsco, -timui, v. a. 3 *greatly dread.*
ex-tinguo, -tinxi, -tinctum, v. a. 3 *quench, annul.*
extortor, -ōris, m. *robber.* [A nonce word.]
extra, prep. *except.*
ex-traho, -trāxi, -trāctum, v. a. 3 *rescue.*
extrārius, -a, -um, *strange, stranger in blood.*
ex-trūdo, -trūsi, -trūsum, v. a. 3 *thrust out.*

fābula, -ae, f. *story, idle story.*
fābulor, v. dep. 1 *talk.*
facēsso, -i, -ītum, v. n. 3 *go away.*
facies, -ēi and -ē, f. *face.*
facilis, -e, *easy.*
facinus, -oris, n. *deed, fact.*
facio, fēci, factum, v. a. 3 *make, do, compose, give.*
faeneror, v. dep. 1 *lend at interest;* **faenerātus**, *lent at interest.*
faenus, -oris, n. *interest.*
fallācia, -ae, f. *trickery.*
fallo, fefelli, falsum, v. a. 3 *deceive, am unseen by.*
falsus, -a, -um, *untrue.*
fāma, -ae, f. *reputation, what the world says.*
fames, -is (abl. famē), f. *hunger, starving.*
familia, -ae, f. *household, family.*
familiāris, -e, *of the household* or *family, intimate.*
familiāritas, -ātis, f. *intimacy.*
faxim, aorist optative of **facio**, used as **faciam** (subj.).
faxo, aorist subjunctive of **facio**, used as future indicative.
fere, adv. *mostly.*
ferio, percussi, percussum, ferire, v. a. 4 *hit.*
ferme, adv. *almost, nearly.*
fero, tuli, lātum, ferre, v. a. irreg. *bear, bring, get.*
fidēlis, -e, *trustworthy, faithful.*
fides, -ēi and -ē, f. *trustworthiness, confidence, promise, honour* (as a quality).
fidicina, -ae, f. *cittern-player.*
fīlia, -ae, f. *daughter.*
fīlius, -li, m. *son.*
fīnis, -is, m. (sometimes f. in sing.) *end.*
fīo, factus sum, fieri: used as passive of **facio**.
flāgitium, -ti, n. *deed of wickedness.*
fleo, flēui, flētum, v. n. 2 *weep.*
foras, adv. *out, out o' doors.*
foris, -is, f. *door.*
foris, adv. *out through the doors, out o' doors.*
forma, -ae, f. *shape, beauty.*
fors, fortis, f. *chance, the goddess Chance;* **Fors Fortuna**, *the goddess Luck.*
forsitan, adv. *it may be that.*
fortasse, adv. *perhaps.*
forte, adv. *as it happens, as it happened, as may happen.*
fortis, -e, *stalwart.*
fortitūdo, -inis, f. *stalwartness, hardihood.*
fortūna, -ae, f. *luck* (see also **Fors**).

fortūnātus, -a, -um, *lucky*.
forum, -i, n. *market-place, piazza*.
frāter, -tris, m. *brother, first cousin*.
fremo, fremui, fremitum, v. n. 3 *rage*.
frētus, -a, -um, *relying*.
frīgeo, v. n. 2 *am cold*.
frūctus, -us and -uis and -i, m. *profit, returns*.
fruor, frūctus sum, v. dep. 3 *enjoy*.
frūstra, adv. *without effect*.
fuga, -ae, f. *flight*.
fugio, fūgi, fugitum, v. n. 3 *run away, flee*.
fugitans, gen. -āntis, *inclined to shun*.
fugitīuos, -a, -om, *a runaway*.
fugito, v. a. 1 *avoid, skulk from*.
fungor, fūnctus sum, v. dep. 3 *perform*.
fūnus, -eris, n. *funeral*.
fūrtum, -i, n. *theft*.

gallīna, -ae, f. *hen*.
garrio, v. n. 4 *talk nonsense*.
gaudeo, gāuīsus sum, v. n. 2 *rejoice*.
gaudium, -di, n. *joy*.
genius, -i, m. *desire* or *capacity for enjoyment*.
gens, gentis, f. *tribe*; **minime gentium**, *never in the world*.
genus, -eris, n. *kin, kinship*.
gero, gessi, gestum, v. a. 3 *transact, do*.
gestio, v. n. 4 *am eager*.
gestus, -us, m. *bearing*.
gladiātōrius, -a, -um, *of a swashbuckler*.
gnātus, -i, m. *son*.
gradus, -us, m. *step*.
grandis, -e *big*; **grandior**, *advanced in years*.
grātia, -ae, f. *gratitude, esteem, favour*.
grātiae, -ārum, f. *thanks*; **gratiis**, *without cost*.
grauis, -e, *heavy, serious, intolerable*.
grex, gregis, m. *troupe*.
gynaecēum, -i, n. *women's apartments*.

habeo, v. a. 2 *have, wear, marry, feel* (of gratitude), v. n. *be*.
habito, v. n. 1 *dwell, live*.
haereo, haesi, haesum, v. n. 2 *stick, am in a difficulty*.
haesito, v. n. 1 *stick*.
hahahae, the sound of a laugh.
hariolor, v. dep. 1 (*am a soothsayer* or *diviner*), *talk nonsense*.
hariolus, -i, m. *soothsayer, diviner*.
haruspex, -icis, m. *soothsayer, diviner*.
hau, haud, adv. *not*.
heia, interj. *my word!*
hem, interj. *what! eh? look here!*
hercle, interj. passing into an adverb, *by Jove! on my word! certainly* (not used by women).
heri, adv. (originally locative) *yesterday*.
heus, interj. *hi you! hi there! I say!*
hic, haec, hoc, dem. pron. *this, the former, the next*.
hic, adv. *here, hereupon*.
hinc, adv. *from here, from hence*.
hoc, pron. passing into an adverb, *to this place, here* (of motion).

hodie, adv. *to-day*, but more often an emphasizing particle in actual or virtual questions (377 note).

homo, -inis, usually m. *human being*, *man*, *fellow*.

honeste, adv. *creditably*, *respectably*.

honos, -ōris, m. *respect for*, *credit*, *good name*.

hōra, -ae, f. *hour*.

horridus, -a, -um, *rough*, *unkempt*.

hospes, -itis, c. *stranger*, *foreign friend*.

huc, pronoun passing into an adverb, *to this place*, *here* (of motion).

hui, interj. *the sound of a whistle*.

iam, adv. *by now*, *at once*, *soon* (with future vb.), *now even*, *already*, *any longer* (with negative).

ibi, adv. *there*, *thereupon*.

idem, eadem, idem, pronoun of identity, *the same*.

idōneus, -a, -um, *fit*.

igitur, adv. *therefore*.

ignōbilis, -e, *low-born*.

ignōro, v. a. 1 *am ignorant of*, *ignore*.

ignōsco, ignōui, ignōtum, v. a. 3 *forgive* (a fault).

ignōtus, -a, -um, *unknown*.

ilicet (perhaps for **irlicet**, i.e. **ire licet**, *you may go*), *all's up*, *it's all over*.

ilico (in loco), *directly*, *immediately* (of time or place).

ille, illa, illud, dem. pron. *that*, *the other*, *the former*.

illi, illic, adv. (locative), *in that matter*, *there*.

illic (ille + ce), emphasized form of **ille**.

illuc, pronoun passing into adverb, *to that place*, *there* (of motion).

immo, adv. *no*, *no indeed*, *on the contrary*, *yes indeed*.

im-mūto, v. a. 1 *change*.

impendeo, -pendi, -pensum, v. a. 2 *overhang*, *am imminent for*.

imperium, -ri, n. *supreme command*, *command*.

im-petro, v. a. 1 *gain by asking*.

impluuium, impluui, n. *impluvium*, *the rain-basin* (in the ātrium or courtyard).

in, prep. *into*, *for*, *in*.

inaudīui (not used in the present), v. a. 4 *have heard an hint of*, *have an inkling of*.

in-cendo, -di, -sum, v. a. 3 *set afire*, *inflame*.

in-cepto, v. a. 1 *undertake*.

incertus, -a, -um, *doubtful*.

in-cido, -cidi, -cāsum, v. n. 3 *fall into*.

in-cipio, -cēpi, -ceptum, v. a. 3 *undertake*.

incōgitans, gen. -āntis, *thoughtless*.

incommodum, -i, n. *unpleasantness*.

inconstāntia, -ae, f. *shiftiness*.

incrēdibilis, -e, *past belief*.

in-cūso, v. a. 1 *accuse*.

inde, pronoun and adv. *from him*, *from her*, *from it*, *from them*, *from that place*, *from thence*.

indico, v. a. 1 *inform*, *disclose*.

indictus, -a, -um, *unsaid*, *retracted*.

indignus, -a, -um, *unfit*, *monstrous*, *unworthy*.

indīligenter, adv. *carelessly*.
indōtāta, fem. adj. *undowered, a wife without a dowry*.
in-eo, -ii, -itum, -īre, v. n. irreg. *enter, go into*.
ineptio, v. n. 4 *talk like a fool* (only present tense).
ineptus, -a, -um, *foolish*.
inexōrābilis, -e, *not to be won over by entreaties, stubborn*.
infectus, -a, -um, *undone*.
infēlix, gen. -īcis, *unlucky, wretched*.
inferus, -a, -um, *of the lower world*.
infirmus, -a, -um, *unsound*.
infortūnium, -ni, n. *misfortune*.
ingenium, -ni, n. *nature, character, bent*.
ingenuos, -a, -om, *gentlemanly, free-born*.
ingrātiis, adv. (abl.), *against one's will, willy-nilly*.
inhūmānus, -a, -um, *inhuman*.
in-icio, -iēci, -iectum, v. a. 3 *throw into, put into*.
inīquos, -a, -om, *unfair*.
initio, v. a. 1 *initiate*.
iniūria, -ae, f. *wrong, assault, action for assault*.
iniussu, adv. (abl.), *without orders*.
inlīberāliter, adv. *in an ungentlemanly way*.
inmerito, adv. (abl.), *undeservedly*.
inopia, -ae, f. *lack of means*.
inops, gen. -opis, *without means*.
inparātus, -a, -um, *unprepared, unready*.
inpedio, v. a. 4 *entangle*.
in-pello, -puli, -pulsum, v. a. 3 *drive on, drive into*.
in-pendeo, -di, -sum, v. a. 2 *overhang, impend*.
in-petro, v. a. 1 *gain by request*.
in-pingo, -pēgi, -pāctum, v. a. 3 *hurl against*.
in-pōno, -posui, -positum, v. a. 3 *put upon*.
inprōuisus, -a, -um, *unforeseen;* **de inprōuiso**, *unexpectedly*.
inprūdens, gen. -ntis, *unforeseeing, careless, unaware*.
inpudens, gen. -ntis, *shameless*.
inpūrātus, -a, -um, *unclean, vile*.
inpūrus, -a, -um, *foul*.
inquam, v. irreg. and defective, *say* (in quotation or in emphasis).
in-rīdeo, -rīsi, -rīsum, v. a. 2 *laugh at*.
inrīto, v. a. 1 *anger, provoke*.
inritus, -a, -um, *unratified, retracted*.
in-sānio, v. n. 4 *am mad, make extravagant demands*.
insciens, gen. -ntis, *ignorant, foolish*.
inscītia, -ae, f. *lack of skill, foolish*.
insidiae, -ārum, f. *ambush, ambuscade, snare*.
in-simulo, v. a. 1 *accuse*.
in-sisto, -stiti, -stitum, v. n. 3 *set about, begin*.
instīgo, v. a. 1 *goad on*.
in-stituo, -ui, -ūtum, v. a. 3 *set in place, set in order*.
in-sto, -stiti, v. n. 1 *am pressing*.
in-struo, -strūxi, -strūctum, v. a. 3 *draw up*.
in-sum, -fui, -esse, v. n. *am in*.
integer, -gra, -grum, *undamaged;* **de integro**, *afresh, freely;* **in integrum**, *to its former state*.

intel-lego, -lēxi, -lēctum, v. a. 3 *understand.*

inter-cēdo, -cessi, -cessum, v. n. 3 *pass between, subsist between.*

inter-dīco, -dixi, -dictum, v. a. 3 *forbid.*

interea, adv. *after a time, on one occasion, at times, meantime.*

in-tero, -trīui, -trītum, v. a. 3 *crumble, pound.*

inter-uenio, -uēni, -uentum, v. n. 4 *come in upon.*

intro, adv. *to the inside, indoors* (of motion).

intrō-dūco, -dūxi, -dūctum, v. a. 3 *introduce.*

intus, adv. *inside, indoors.*

in-uenio, -uēni, -uentum, v. a. 4 *light upon, find.*

in-uestīgo, v. a. 1 *trace out.*

inuidia, -ae, f. *jealousy, envy.*

inuītus, -a, -um, *unwilling.*

ioculāris, -e, *sporting, sportive, laughable.*

ipse and **ipsus**, -a, -um, dem. pron. *self, myself,* etc.

īrācundia, -ae, f. *passionateness.*

īrāscor, īrātus sum, v. dep. 3 *grow angry.*

is, ea, id, dem. pron. *that* [used also where we say 'he,' 'she,' etc.].

iste, ista, istud, dem. pron. *that, that of yours, this.*

istic, istac, istuc (iste + ce), emphatic form of **iste**.

istōrsum, adv. *in this* or *that direction* (to which the speaker points).

ita, adv. *thus, so, so much, on this condition, yes.*

item, adv. *also.*

iter, itineris (earlier also *iteris*), n. *way, journey.*

itidem, adv. *in the same way.*

iubeo, iūssi, iūssum, v. a. 2 *bid, request.*

iūdex, -ĭcis, c. *judge.*

iūdicium, -ci, n. *judgement.*

iūrgium, -gi, n. *squabble* (with words).

ius, iūris, n. *law, law-court.*

iūstus, -a, -um, *just, right.*

lacēsso, -īui and -i, -ītum, v. a. 3 *provoke.*

lacruma, -ae, f. *tear.*

laedo, -si, -sum, v. a. 3 *hit at, try to hurt, hurt.*

laetus, -a, -um, (well-tilled) *merry, glad.*

lāmentor, v. dep. 1 *bewail.*

later, -eris, m. *brick.*

laudo, v. a. 1 *praise;* **laudo**, *bravo!*

lauo, lāui, lautum, *wash, wash clean, bath.*

lēctus, -a, -um, *pickt, choice.*

lēnis, -e, *mild.*

lēno, -ōnis, m. *slave-dealer, pander.*

lepidus, -a, -um, *jolly.*

leuis, -e, *light, trifling.*

lēx, lēgis, f. *condition, statute, law, rule.*

līberālis, -e, *with the mind of a gentleman or gentlewoman.*

licet, v. impers. 2 *it is allowed, it is lawful.*

lītes, -ium (pl. of *lis*), f. *a row* (slang use).

loco, v. a. 1 *settle in marriage.*

locus, -i, m. (pl. also *loca*, n.)

time, *place*, *room*, *state* or *condition*.
logi, acc. logos, m. λόγοι, *empty words*.
longus, -a, -um, *long*.
loquor, locūtus sum, v. dep. 3 *speak*.
lubens, gen. -ntis, *glad*.
lubenter, adv. *gladly*.
lubet, lubuit and lubitum est, v. impers. 2 *it just pleases*.
lucrum, -i, n. *gain*.
lūdificor, v. dep. 1 *make game of*.
lūdo, -si, -sum, v. a. and n. 3 *play*, *mock*, *befool*.
lūdus, -i, m. *game*, *music-school*, *entertainment*.
lupus, -i, m. *wolf*.
lutum, -i, n. *mud*.

macto, v. a. 1 *immolate*, *ruin*.
magis, adv. comparative of **māgno opere**, *more*.
magister, -tri, m. *master*, *director*.
magistrātus, -us, m. *official*, *judge*.
māgnificentia, -ae, f. *bragging*, *bombast*.
māgnus, -a, -um, *great*.
male, adv. *badly*.
maledīctum, -i, n. *hard word*, *curse*.
malefacio, -fēci, -factum, v. n. 3 *do harm*, *do wrong*.
malitia, -ae, f. *spite*, *ill-will*.
mālo, mālui, mālle, v. irreg. *prefer*.
malum, i, n. *misfortune*, *punishment*; **malum** (acc. used interjectionally), *the plague!*
malus, -a, -um, *bad*.
mando, v. a. 1 *intrust*.
māne, adv. (locative), *in the morning*.
maneo, mansi, mansum, v. a. and n. 2 *wait for*, *wait*.
mansio, -ōnis, f. *stopping*.
manus, -us, f. *hand*.
māter, -tris, f. *mother*.
māxume, adv. sup. of **māgno opere**, *most of all*, *in the highest degree*, *most certainly*.
medeor, v. dep. 2 *heal*.
meditor, v. dep. 1 *rehearse*.
medius, -a, -um, *middle*; **in medio**, *open to all*.
memini, v. preteritive, 3 *remember*.
memoria, -ae, f. *memory*.
memoriter, adv. *word for word*, *without a mistake*.
mens, mentis, f. *mind*.
mensis, -is, m. *month*.
merces, -ēdis, f. *pay*, *reward*.
mercor, v. dep. 1 *market*, *traffic*.
mereor, v. dep. 2 *deserve*.
meretrix, -īcis, f. *harlot*.
meritum, -i, n. *desert*.
merus, -a, -um, *unmixt*.
metuo, -ui, -ūtum (*Lucr.*), v. a. 3 *am apprehensive of*.
meus, -a, -um, *my*, *mine*.
mīles, -itis, m. *soldier*, *officer*.
mīluos, -i, m. *kite* (the red kite).
mina, -ae, f. (μνᾶ), *mina* (about £4).
minime, adv. sup. of **paullum**, *least of all*, *not at all*.
minitor, v. dep. 1 *threaten*.
minuo, -ui, -utum, v. a. 3 *diminish*, *lessen*.
minus, adv. comp. of **paullum**, *less*, *too little*, *not*.

mīrificus, -a, -um, *astonishing*.
mīror, v. dep. 1 (stand agape at) *wonder*, *wonder at*.
mīrus, -a, -um, *wonderful*.
miser, -era, -erum, *wretched*.
miserandus, -a, -um, *to be pitied*, *lamentable*.
miseret, miseruit and miseritum est, v. impers. 2 *it strikes with pity*.
misericordia, -ae, f. *pity*, *compassion*.
mitto, mīsi, missum, v. a. 3 *send*, *dismiss*, *drop*, *make a present*; **missum facio**, *dismiss*.
modeste, adv. *with moderation*.
modo, adv. *just now*, *only*, *just*, *provided that*.
modus, -i, m. *manner*.
molestus, -a, -um, *troublesome*.
mollio, v. a. 4 *soften*, *mollify*.
molo, -ui, -itum, v. a. 3 *grind*.
moneo, v. a. 2 *remind*, *advise*.
monitor, -ōris, m. *superintendent*.
mons, montis, m. *mountain*.
monstrum, -i, n. *portent*, *prodigy*.
morbus, -i, m. *illness*.
morior, mortuos sum, mori (sometimes morīri), v. dep. 3 *die*.
moror, v. dep. 1 *delay*, *linger*, *hinder*.
mors, mortis, f. *death*.
mos, mōris, m. *custom*.
moueo, mōui, mōtum, v. a. 2 *move*.
mox, adv. *after an interval*, *later on*, *presently*; **quam mox**, *how long will it be before*.
mulier, -eris, f. *woman*, *dame*.
muliercula, -ae, f. *little woman*, *wretched woman*.
multimodis, adv. *very*, *very much*.
multus, -a, -um, *much*, *many*.
mūnus, -eris, n. *gift*.

nam, interrogative particle, proclitic, enclitic, or independent: used also pleonastically with interrogative pronouns.
nam, conj. *for*.
nancīscor, nactus sum, v. dep. 3 *light on*, *find*.
narro, v. a. 1 *relate*.
nātālis, -e, *of birth*.
nauta, -ae, m. *sailor*.
-ne, interrogative enclitic, often shortened to **n**: used also with the exclamatory infinitive.
ne, adv. *not*: used in imperative, prohibitive, final and restrictive sentences, and after a verb of fearing where we use 'that.'
necesse, n. adj. *inevitable*.
neglegentia, -ae, f. *neglect*.
nego, v. a. and n. 1 *say no*, *deny* [neg + aio, but brought into the first conjugation].
negōtium, -ti, n. *business*, *affair*.
nēmo, acc. nēminem (gen. and abl. usually borrowed from **nūllus**), c. *no one*, *no man*.
nempe, adv. *of course*, *I presume*.
neque, adv. + conj. *neither*, *nor*, *and not* (519 note).
nequeo, -īre, v. n. irreg. *cannot*, *am unable*.
neruos, -i, m. (sinew) *fetter*.
nēscio, v. a. 4 *do not know*.
nex, necis, f. *violent death*.
ni, adv. *not* (obsolescent except in the phrase **quid ni** and in hypothetical clauses with **si** implied, where it comes to be regarded as an equivalent for **nisi**).

nihil, nil, nihili, n. *nothing* (142 note).
nisi, adv. + conj. *if not, unless*: adv. *only* (475 note).
nōlo, nōlui, nōlle (ne + uolo), v. irreg. *am unwilling*; **noli** and **nolite** with inf. *do not*.
non, adv. *not*.
nōndum, adv. *not yet*.
nōsmet, emphatic form of **nos**.
nōster, -tra, -trum, poss. pron. *our, ours*.
nōstrapte, emphatic form of **nostra**.
nōtus, -a, -um (nōsco), *known*.
nōui, nōueram and nōram, nōsse, preteritive v. *know, am acquainted with*.
nouos, -a, -om, *new, novel*.
noxia, -ae, f. *fault, blame*.
nūbo, -psi, -ptum, v. n. 3 (put on a veil) *am married*.
nūdus, -a, -um, *bare, naked*.
nūllus, -a, -um, *no, none*; **nūllus sum**, *I am done for* (179 note).
num, interrogative particle expecting a negative answer.
numerus, -i, m. *number*.
nummus, -i, m. *coin, franc* (δράχμη).
numquam, adv. *never* (121 note).
nūnc, adv. *now, as it is*.
nūntio, v. a. 1 *bring news of, announce*.
nūntius, acc. -um, m. *messenger, message*.
nusquam, adv. *nowhere*.
nūtrix, -īcis, f. *nurse*.

ob, prep. *meeting, on account of, for* (of money borrowed on mortgage).
ob-eo, -ii, -itum, -ire, v. irreg. *die* (*mortem* understood).
ob-icio, -iēci, -iectum, v. a. 3 *throw in the way*.
ob-iūrgo, v. a. 1 *rail at*.
ob-lecto, v. a. 1 *charm, delight*.
ob-secro, v. a. 1 *entreat*.
ob-stipēfacio, -fēcī, -fectum, v. a. 3 *strike dumb*.
ob-stipēsco, -stipui, v. n. 3 *am dazed, grow dumb*.
obuiam, adv. *meeting, to meet*.
oc-cido, -cidi, v. n. 3 *die*.
oc-cīdo, -cīsi, -cīsum, v. a. 3 *kill*.
oc-cipio, -cēpi, -ceptum, v. n. 3 *begin*.
occupo, v. a. 1 *seize beforehand, preoccupy*.
ōcius, adv. comp. *pretty quickly*.
oculus, -i, m. *eye*.
odiōsus, -a, -um, *distasteful, boring*.
odium, -i, n. *dislike, annoying ways, boring ways*.
of-fendo, -di, -sum, v. a. 3 *light on, find*.
officium, -ci, n. *duty*.
og-gannio, v. n. 4 *growl at*.
oh, interj. *oh! oh ho!*
ŏhe, interj. *oh dear! oh bother!*
oiei, interj. *oh come!*
olim, adv. *at that time, at the time, in time past*.
o-mitto, -mīsi, -missum, v. a. 3 *let go*.
omnis, -e, *all, every, every kind of*.
onero, v. a. 1 *load*.
onus, -eris, n. *load, burden*.
opem (acc.), opis, f. *help*.
operae, -ae, f. *doing, work, help*.
operio, -perui, -pertum, v. a. 4 *shut*.

opes, -um, f. *means.*
opīnor, v. dep. 1 *think, take it that.*
opitulor, v. dep. 1 *give help.*
oportet, v. impers. 2 *it befits.*
op-perior, -pertus, v. dep. 4 *wait for.*
oppido, adv. *very, very much so.* [Perhaps **ob pedum**, *on the level,* i.e. *plainly.*]
op-pōno, -posui, -positum, v. a. 3 *mortgage.*
opportūne, adv. *at the right moment.*
op-primo, -pressi, -pressum, v. a. 3 *gag.*
op-tingo, -tigi, -tāctum, v. n. 3 *befall.*
opto, v. a. 1 *desire* (especially of what is not very likely).
optume, adv. sup. of **bene**, *in the best way, excellently.*
op-tundo, -tudi, -tūnsum and -tūsum, v. a. 3 *deafen.*
opus, -eris, n. (work) *farm-work.*
opus, n. *need.*
ōrātio, -onĭs, f. *speech, style.*
ordo, -inis, m. *order.*
ornātus, -a, -um (orno), *well-equipt, illustrious.*
ōro, v. a. 1 (speak), *pray, plead* (a cause).
os, ōris, n. *mouth, face.*
os-tendo, -di, -sum, v. a. 3 *show.*
ōstium, -ti, n. *door.*
ōtiōsus, -a, -um, *unoccupied.*
ōtium, -ti, n. *repose, time for repose.*

pāctum, -i, n. *way, manner.*
paedagōgus, -i, m. *slave in charge of children, male nurse.*
paene, adv. *almost.*
paenitet, v. impers. 2 *it dissatisfies.*
palaestra, -ae, f. *wrestling-school, gymnasium.*
palam, adv. *openly.*
pallium, -i, n. *oblong piece of cloth used as a cloak.*
palma, -ae, f. *palm, prize.*
pando, pandi, pansum and pāssum, v. a. 3 *spread out.*
par, gen. paris, *equal, right.*
parasītus, -i, m. *adventurer, sponger.*
parco, parsi (obsolescent) and peperci, v. n. 3 *am sparing.*
parens, -ntis, c. (mother), *parent.*
pario, peperi, partum, v. a. 3 *bear* (a child), *get, save* (money): **parta**, *savings.*
pariter, adv. *equally.*
paro, v. a. 1 *make ready, set about.*
partes, -ium, f. *rôle, part in a play.*
parum, adv. *very little, too little.*
parumper, adv. *for a short time.*
paruos, -a, -om, *little, small.*
pāsco, pāui, pāstum, v. a. 3 *feed.*
pater, -tris, m. *father.*
paternus, -a, -um, *of a father, fatherly.*
patior, pati, passus sum, v. dep. 3 *endure, suffer, put up with.*
patrōcinor, v. dep. 1 *champion, hold a brief for.*
patrōnus, -i, m. *champion.*
patruos, -i, m. *father's brother, uncle.*
pauci, -ae, -a, *few.*
paueo, pāui, v. n. 2 *quake with fear.*
paullo, paulo, adv. *with a little, by a little.*

paullulum, paululum, adv. as n. noun, *a very little.*

paullum, adv. and adv. as n. noun, *a little.*

pauper, gen. -eris, *of small means.*

paupertas, -ātis, f. *scanty means.*

pauxillulum, adv. as n. noun, *a very very little.*

peccātum, -i, n. *fault, peccadillo.*

pecco, v. n. 1 *am in fault.*

pecūnia, -ae, f. *money.*

pedetemptim, adv. *step by step, gingerly.*

pel-licio, -lexi, -lectum, v. a. 3 *allure.*

penātes, -ium, m. (gods of the larder), *household gods.*

pendeo, pependi, pensum, v. n. 2 *hang.*

per, prep. *through, by means of, because of, in the name of.*

percārus, -a, -um, *very dear.*

percontor, v. dep. 1 *question.*

perdite, adv. *consumedly, desperately.*

per-do, -didi, -ditum, v. a. 3 *ruin, destroy, forget.* [The passive is **pereo.**]

peregre, adv. *abroad, from abroad.*

per-eo, -ii, -itum, -īre, v. n. irreg. *am ruined.*

per-ficio, -fēci, -fectum, v. a. 3 *complete, accomplish.*

pergo, perrexi, perrectum, v. n. 3 *go, go on to, persist in.*

perīclum, -i, n. *trial, law-suit, peril, danger.*

perlīberālis, -e, *very lady-like.*

perperam, adv. *wrongly, falsely.*

per-sequor, -secūtus sum, v. dep. 3 *follow after.*

per-spicio, -spexi, -spectum, v. a. 3 *observe closely, see clearly.*

per-suādeo, -suāsi, -suāsum, v. n. 2 *persuade.*

per-timēsco, -timui, v. a. 3 *greatly fear.*

per-uenio, -uēni, -uentum, v. n. 4 *arrive.*

pes, pedis, m. *foot.*

peto, petīui and petii, petītum, v. a. 3 *look for, try to get.*

phalerātus, -a, -um, *with fine trappings, fine, showy.* (**phalerae** were metal disks borne on the standards and worn by soldiers as a decoration of honour.)

piget, v. impers. 2 *it sickens.*

pignus, -oris, n. *pledge;* **pignori oppōno**, *mortgage.*

pistrīnum, -i, *mill.*

plācābilis, -e, *easily appeased, able to appease.*

placeo, v. n. 2 *please.*

placide, adv. *calmly, gently.*

plāco, v. a. 1 *appease.*

plāga (Doric πλαγά), -ae, f. *stripe, blow.*

plāne, adv. *clearly, plainly.*

platea (πλατεῖα), -ae, f. *street.*

plaudo, -si, -sum, v. n. 3 *clap my hands.*

plēctor (πλήττω), v. n. 3 *am punisht* (usually for another's fault).

plērīque, -aeque, -aque, *very many, most.*

plērumque, adv. *mostly.*

plōro, v. n. 1 *wail, lament* (later also transitive).

plūrimum, sup. adv. *mostly.*

plūsculus, -a, -um, *a little more.*

poēta (ποιητής), -ae, m. *poet.*
pol, interj. passing into adv. *on my word! I vow! I assure you!*
polliceor, v. dep. 2 *promise.*
pollicitātio, -ōnis, f. *promise.*
pollicitor, v. dep. 1 *promise.*
pōno, posui, positum, v. a. 3 *lay down, lay aside, place, suppose, grant.*
populāris, -is, m. *member of the same country or deme, countryman.*
populus, -i, m. *people.*
porro, adv. *further, thereupon, henceforth.*
portitor, -ōris, m. *harbour-official, custom-house officer.*
portus, -us, m. *harbour.*
possiem, pres. subj. of *possum.*
possum, potui, posse, v. irreg. *can, am able.*
post-habeo, v. n. 2 *value less, postpone.*
posthac, adv. *after this time.*
postilla, adv. *after that time.*
postquam, conj. *after, because.*
postrēmo, adv. *last, finally.*
postrīdie, adv. *next day.*
postulo, v. a. 1 *demand.*
potestas, -ātis, f. *legal authority, means.*
potior, potītus sum, potīri, v. dep. 4 (some forms 3), *have possession of, get.*
potis, -is and -e, *able, possible.*
potissimum, sup. adv. *soonest, for choice.*
potius, comp. adv. *rather, sooner.*
pōto, v. n. 1 *tope, tipple.*
prae, adv. *ahead, forward.*
prae-beo (habeo), v. a. 2 *supply, afford.*
praeceps, gen. -ipitis, *headlong, over the cliff.*
prae-dico, v. a. 1 *assert, give us information.*
prae-dīco, -dīxi, -dictum, v. a. 3 *foretell.*
praedium, -di, n. *farm.*
praemium, -mi, n. *prize.*
praesens, gen. -entis, *present, bold, resolute.*
praesentia, -ōrum, n. *present circumstances.*
praesertim, adv. *especially.*
prae-stituo, -ui, -ūtum, v. a. 3 *fix beforehand.*
prae-sto, -stiti, v. n. 1 *am better, excel.*
praesto, adv. *ready, present.*
praeter, prep. *past, beyond, except.*
praeterea, adv. *besides.*
praeter-eo, -ii, -itum, -ire, v. n. irreg. *go by.*
praeter-hac, adv. *beyond this, besides.*
prāuos, -a, -om, *bad.*
precātor, -ōris, m. *intercessor.*
precem (acc.), -is, f. *prayer.*
precor, v. dep. 1 *pray, entreat.*
prēndo (prae-hendo), -di, -sum, v. a. 3 *clutch, seize, catch hold of.*
prīdem, adv. *some time since, hours ago, days ago.*
prīmārius, -a, -um, *of the highest rank* or *character.*
prīmo, adv. *at first.*
prīmum, adv. *first, in the first place.*
prīmus, -a, -um, *first.*
prīncipium, -pi, n. *beginning.*
prior, -us, *earlier, preferred.*
prīuo, v. a. 1 *deprive.*

pro, prep. (before), *in place of*, *on behalf of.*

pro, interj. *oh! shame! oh scandalous!*

probe, adv. *well*, *honestly.*

probrum, -i, n. (disgraceful act), *opprobrium.*

probus, -a, -um, *good*, *honest.*

prō-cūro, v. a. 1 *take care of*, *manage.*

prōd-eo, -ii, -itum, -īre, v. irreg. *go forward*, *go out.*

prō-fero, -tuli, -lātum, -ferre, v. a. irreg. *bring out.*

proficīscor, profectus sum, v. dep. 3 *start*, *set out.*

progenies, -e or -ēi, f. *family.*

prōgnātus, -a, -um, *born.*

pro-hibeo, v. a. 2 *prevent*, *forbid.*

proinde, adv. *just.*

prōlogus (πρόλογος), -i, m. *prologue.*

prō-loquor, -locūtus sum, v. dep. 3 *speak out.*

prō-mereor, v. dep. 2 *deserve beforehand*, *deserve.*

prō-mitto, -mīsi, -missum, v. a. 3 *promise.*

propemodum, adv. *nearly*, *nearly right.*

propero, v. n. 1 *hasten.*

propior, -us, *nearer.*

propitius, -a, -um, *favourable.*

propter, prep. *because of.*

prōtēlo, v. a. 1 *rout.*

prōtinam, adv. (straight forward), *at once.*

prō-uideo, -uīdi, -uīsum, v. a. 2 *foresee*, *provide for.*

prō-uincia, -ae, f. *magistrate's sphere of duty*, *office.*

proxumus, -a, -um, *nearest*, *next*, *next of kin.*

publicitus, adv. *at the cost of the state.*

publicus, -a, -um, *public.*

pudet, v. impers. 2 *shame takes.*

pudor, -ōris, m. *modesty*, *shame.*

puellula, -ae, f. *slip of a girl.*

puer, -eri, m. *boy*, *page-boy*, *slave* (cf. garçon).

pūgnus, -i, m. *fist.*

pulcer, -cra, -crum, *fine*, *beautiful.*

pulcre, adv. *finely.*

pulcritūdo, -inis, f. *beauty.*

punctum, -i, n. *moment.*

pūrgo, v. a. 1 *clear*, *justify:* v. n. *apologize.*

puto, v. a. 1 *think*, *take it that.*

quaero, quaesīui, quaesītum, v. a. 3 *look for*, *inquire about*, *ask for.*

quaeso, v. def. 3 (usually parenthetic) *pray.*

quālis, -e, *of what sort*, *of which sort.*

quam, adv. and conj. *how*, *how much*, *than.*

quando, conj. *when? when*, *because;* enclitic, *ever.*

quandoquidem, conj. *because.*

quantum potest, *as soon as possible.* (The verb is impersonal.)

quantus, -a, -um, *how great? how much? as great as*, *as much as*, *as.*

quantusquantus, -aquanta, -umquantum, *however great.*

quasi, conj. *as if.*

queo, v. irreg. and def. *am able.*

qui, quae, quod, rel. pron. *who*, *which.* Colloquial in questions for *quis.*

qui (abl. of *qui* and *quis*), *how? how*. With an optative verb = *utinam*.
quia, conj. *because*.
quid, interrog. adv. *why?* (acc. of *quis*).
quid? *again, then again* (in enumeration of instances).
quidam, quaedam, quoddam, indef. pron. *an, a*.
quidem, adv. *for sure, indeed*.
quiēsco, -ēui, -ētum, v. n. 3 *grow quiet, am quiet*.
quiētus, -a, -um, *quiet*.
quin (qui + ne), pron. and adv. *who not, which not, why not, for which not*. Used also to emphasize an imperative.
quinque, *five*.
quippe, conj. *for of course*.
quis, quis or quae, quid, interrog. (and exclamatory) pron. *who? what?* **quid!** *how much!*
quis, quae or qua, quid, indef. pron. *any, anyone*.
quisnam: see **nam**.
quisquam, quidquam or quicquam, indef. pron. with actual or implied negative, *any, anyone*.
quisquis, quisquis, quidquid or quicquid, pron. *whoever*.
quīuis, quaeuis, quiduis or quoduis, pron. *any you choose, any and every*.
quo, interrog. and rel. pron. and adv. *to what point? to what place? to which place, to which point*.
quo, adv. (abl. of *qui*), *in order that*.
quoad, *until when*.
quod, conj. (acc. of *qui*), *but*.
quoi = cui: **quoius** = cūius.
quom, conj. (acc. of *qui*), *when, although, whereas*. With *tum* to follow it gets the sense of *not only*.
quōquo, adv. *to whatever place*.
quor (later *cur*), adv. and conj. *where*.

ratio, -ōnis, f. *reckoning, reasoning*.
ratiūncula, -ae, f. *trifling account, small reckoning*.
re-cipio, -cēpi, -ceptum, v. a. 3 *take back, betake, undertake*.
recta, sc. *uia*, adv. (abl.), *directly, in a straight line*.
recte, adv. *rightly, all right*.
rectus, -a, -um, *straight*.
red-do, -didi, -ditum, v. a. 3 *pay back, restore, grant, answer, bring in* (income).
red-dūco, -dūxi, -dūctum, v. a. 3 *lead back*.
red-eo, -ii, -itum, -īre, v. n. irreg. *go back, come to a state, come to a point*.
red-igo, -ēgi, -āctum, v. a. 3 *bring back, reduce*.
re-fello, -felli, v. n. 3 *refute*.
re-fero, rettuli, rellātum (later relātum), referre, v. a. irreg. *repay, send back at*.
rēfert, rettulit, rēferre, v. impers. irreg. *it concerns*.
rēgno, v. a. 1 *am king*.
relicuos, -a, -om, *remaining, remaining over*.
re-linquo, -līqui, -lictum, v. a. 3 *leave*.
remedium, -i, n. *cure, remedy*.
re-mitto, -mīsi, -missum, v. a. 3 *send back*.

re-nūntio, v. a. 1 *send back word of, send word of.*

reor, ratus sum, v. dep. 2 (reckon) *think;* **ratus**, *ratified.*

re-perio, repperi, repertum, v. a. 4 *find* (by search).

re-peto, -petīui, -petītum, v. a. 3 *try to get back, try to recover.*

repudium, -di, n. *renouncement of a marriage contract.*

re-quīro, -quīsīui, -quīsītum, v. a. 3 *look for.*

res, rĕi and rēi, f. *property, interest, matter, affair, business.*

re-scindo, -scidi, -scissum, v. a. 3 *rescind.*

re-scīsco, -scīui and -scii, -scītum, v. a. 3 *get to know.*

re-scrībo, -scrīpsi, -scrīptum, v. a. 3 *re-transfer from one man's account to another's, pay back.*

re-sisto, -stiti, -stitum, v. n. 3 *stop.*

re-spicio, -spexi, -spectum, v. a. and n. *look back at, look back.*

re-spondeo, -spondi, -sponsum, v. a. 2 *answer.*

responsum, -i, n. *answer.*

re-stinguo, -stinxi, -stīnctum, v. a. 3 *quench.*

restis, -is (acc. -im or -em), f. *rope, halter.*

re-stituo, -ui, -ūtum, v. a. 3 *restore.*

re-sto, -stiti, v. n. 3 *remain, am left.*

re-supīno, v. a. 1 *turn back.*

rēte, -is (abl. -e), n. *net.*

re-tineo, -tinui, -tentum, v. a. 2 *hold back.*

re-traho, -trāxi, -trāctum, v. a. 3 *drag back.*

re-uereor, v. dep. 2 *respect.*

re-uertor (re-uortor), -sus -sum, v. dep. (middle) 3 *return.*

re-uoco, v. a. 1 *call back.*

rēx, rēgis, m. *king, patron, great man.*

rīdiculus, -a, -um, *laughable, absurd.*

ringor, rictus sum, v. dep. (middle) 3 *show the teeth.*

rogito, v. a. 1 *ask.*

rogo, v. a. 1 *ask.*

rūfus, -a, -um, *red, red-headed.*

rūmor, -ōris, m. *talk, town-talk.*

rūrsum, adv. *back, in turn.*

rus, rūris, n. *the country.*

sacrifico, v. a. and n. 1 *sacrifice, offer sacrifice.*

saepe, adv. *often.*

saeuidicus, -a, -um, *fierce in tone.*

saeuos, -a, -om, *fierce, grim.*

saltem, adv. *at least.*

salueo, v. n. 2 (am in health): used in salutations in the imperative and phrases such as *saluēre iubeo.*

saluos, -a, -om, *in health, whole and sound.*

salūto, v. a. 1 *greet.*

sāne, adv. *very, it must be allowed.*

sānus, -a, -um, *sane.*

sapiens, gen. -ntis, *wise.*

sapio, -īui and -ii, v. n. 3 *have a taste, am wise.*

sat, satis, adv. *quite, enough.*

satietas, -ātis, f. *one's full.*

satin, satine = *satisne.*

satius, comp. adv. *better.*

scapulae, -ārum, f. *shoulder-blades.*

scelus, -eris, n. *sin, wickedness, crime, wicked things.*

sciens, gen. -ntis, *knowing, skilful.*
scīlicet, adv. *for certain, of course, undoubtedly.*
scīn = *scīsne.*
scio, v. a. 4 *know, know how, can.*
scītum, -i, n. *knowledge.*
scītus, -a, -um, *sensible, good-looking.*
scopulus, -i, m. *rock, crag.*
scrībo, scrīpsi, scrīptum, v. a. 3 *write, compose, bring* (an action).
scrīptūra, -ae, f. *composition, style.*
scrūpulus, -i, m. (small sharp stone), *cause for hesitation, doubt.*
se, reflexive pronoun of the 3rd pers. *himself* etc.
sector, v. dep. 1 *follow, pursue.*
secundus, -a, -um, *favourable.*
secus, adv. *otherwise.*
sed, conj. *but.*
sedeo, sēdi, v. n. 2 *sit.*
sēdulo, adv. *diligently, zealously.*
semper, adv. *always.*
senectus, -ūtis, f. *old age.*
senex, senis, m. *old man, old gentleman.*
sententia, -ae, f. *judgement, opinion:* **ex sententia**, *satisfactorily, satisfactory.*
sentio, sēnsi, sēnsum, v. a. 4 *feel, am aware of, am troubled by.*
sepelio, -īui, sepultum, v. a. 4 *bury.*
sequor, secūtus sum, v. dep. 3 *go with, attend, follow.*
seruio, v. n. 4 *am a slave.*
seruitus, -ūtis, f. *slavery.*
seruo, v. a. 1 *keep, save.*
seruos, -i, m. *slave.*
sescenti, -ae, -a, *six hundred, any number of.*
si, conj. *if, if as is the case.*
sic, adv. *so.*
siem, sies, siet, sient: pres. subj. of *sum.*
silentium, -i, n. *silence, absence of noise.*
sileo, v. n. 2 *am silent, make no noise.*
similis, -e, *like.*
simul, *at once.*
simultās, -ātis, f. *quarrel.*
sīn, conj. *but if.*
sine, prep. *without.*
singulātim, adv. *one by one.*
sino, sīui, situm, v. a. 3 *place, leave alone, leave, allow.*
siquidem, conj. *yes if.*
sis = si uis, *if you please.*
sobrīnus, -i, m. *cousin-german on the mother's side.*
sōdes = si audes, *if you please.*
soleo, solitus sum, v. n. 2 *have a way of, am accustomed to.*
sollicitūdo, -inis, f. *anxiety.*
soluo, solui, solutum, v. a. 3 *loose, pay.*
sōlus, -a, -um, *alone, only, desert.*
somnium, -ni, n. *dream, unreality.*
spatium, -i, n. *room, time.*
sperno, sprēui, sprētum, v. a. 3 *become estranged from.*
spes, spēī, f. *hope.*
spondeo, spopondi, sponsum, v. a. 2 *betroth.*
statim, adv. *on each occasion, regularly.*
sterculīnum, -i, n. *muck-heap.*
sto, steti, stātum, v. n. 1 *stand, am successful, support* (with *cum*).

strēnuos, -a, -om, *diligent*, *zealous*.
studeo, v. n. 2 *am zealous*.
studium, -i, n. *calling*, *profession*, *zeal*.
stultitia, -ae, f. *foolishness*, *folly*.
stultus, -a, -um, *foolish*.
suādeo, suāsi, suāsum, v. n. 2 *am urgent with*, *urge*.
suāuis, -e, *sweet*, *pleasant*.
subcenturiātus, -i, m. *soldier in reserve*.
sub-icio, -iēci, -iectum, v. a. 3 *whisper*, *prompt*.
subito, adv. *suddenly*.
sub-olet, v. impers. 2 *there is an inkling*.
sub-uenio, -uēni, -uentum, v. n. 4 *help*.
sūdo, v. n. 1 *sweat*.
sūmma, -ae, f. *sum total*.
sūmmus, -a, -um, *highest*, *greatest*, *very great*.
sūmo (sub + emo), sūmpsi, sūmptum, v. a. 3 *take*, *borrow*.
sūmptus, -i, and -us, m. *cost*.
suo, sūtum, v. a. 3 *sew*, *stitch*, *set a trap*.
suos, -a, -om, *own* (his, her, its, their).
supellex, supellectilis, f. *furniture*.
superbe, adv. *haughtily*, *harshly*.
super-sum, -fui, -esse, v. n. irreg. *am over*, *am superfluous*.
supplex, gen. -icis, *suppliant*.
supplicium, -ci, n. *punishment*.
sus-cēnseo, v. n. 2 *am angry*.
sus-cipiō, -cēpi, -ceptum, v. a. 3 *undertake*, *take up*, *acknowledge as a child*.
sus-pendo, -di, -sum, v. a. 3 *hang up*, *elevate*; **suspenso gradu**, *on tip-toe*.

taceo, v. n. 1 *hold my tongue*.
taedet, v. impers. 2 *it bores*, *it sickens*.
talentum, τάλαντον, -i, n. *talent* (about £250).
tam, adv. *as much*, *so much*, *so*, *as well*.
tamen, conj. *nevertheless*, *yet*.
tametsi, conj. *even although*.
tandem, adv. *at length*, *at the worst*, *pray*.
tango, tetigi, tāctum, v. a. 3 *touch*.
tanto opere, adv. *so much*.
tantummodo, adv. *only*.
tantundem, adv. *just so much*.
tantus, -a, -um, *so much*, *so great*, *as much*, *as great*.
tēgulae, -ārum, f. *tiles*.
temere, adv. (old abl.), *at random*, *rashly*, *without cause*, *by chance*.
temperans, gen. -ntis, *heedful*.
tempto, v. a. 1 *test*.
tempus, -oris, n. *time*, *fitting time*, *opportunity*.
tendo, tetendi, tentum, v. a. 3 *stretch*, *set* (a net).
teneo, tenui, v. a. 2 *hold*, *understand*.
tennitur, colloquial form of *tenditur*.
tenuis, -e, *thin*, *meagre*.
tenuiter, adv. *meagrely*.
testimōnium, -i, n. *evidence*.
testis, -is, c. *witness*.
tētē, emphatic form of *te*; cf. *sēse*.
timeo, v. a. 2 *fear*.
timidus, -a, -um, *timid*.

timor, -ōris, m. *fear.*
tolero, v. a. 1 *bear, put up with.*
tonstrīna, -ae, f. *barber's shop.*
tōtus, -a, -um, *whole.*
trācto, v. a. 1 *handle.*
trā-do, -didi, -ditum, v. a. 3 *transfer.*
tranquillus, -a, -um, *calm;* **tranquillum**, *calm water.*
trans-do = *trado.*
trans-eo, -ii, -itum, -īre, v. n. irreg. *go across, cross.*
trans-igo, -ēgi, -āctum, v. a. 3 *transact.*
tres, tria, *three.*
trīduom, -i, n. *three days.*
trīginta, *thirty.*
trīstis, -e, *out of spirits, glum.*
triumpho, v. n. 1 *win a triumph, triumph.*
tu, personal pron. *you.*
tum, adv. *then, moreover, what is more, what is worse.*
tumultus, -us and -i, m. *uproar, disturbance.*
tuos, -a, -om, *your, yours.*
turba, -ae, f. *disturbance, uproar.*
tūtĕ, emphatic form of *tu* with added particle.
tūtor, v. dep. 1 *guard, protect.*
tūtus, -a, -um, *secure from harm, safe.*

ualeo, v. n. 2 *am in health;* **uale**, **ualēte**, *good-bye.*
uānitas, -ātis, f. *shiftiness, lack of truthfulness.*
uāpulo, v. n. 1 *get a whipping.*
ubi, pron. and adv. rel. and interrog. *with whom, in whom, where, when* (in a case), *in which.*
ueho, uexi, uectum, v. a. 3 *carry.*
uel, adv. and conj. *if you like, either, or* (142 note).
uēndo, -didi, -ditum, v. a. 3 *sell.*
uenia, -ae, f. *leave, permission.*
uenio, uēni, uēntum, v. n. 4 *come.*
uenter, -tris, m. *belly.*
uerbero, -ōnis, m. *one who deserves whipping, rascal.*
uerbum, -i, n. *word;* **uerba do**, *cheat.*
uerēcundus, -a, -um, *bashful, modest.*
uereor, v. a. 2 *fear, respect.*
uēro, conj. *but, in truth.*
uērumtamen, conj. *nevertheless.*
uērus, -a, -um, *true.*
uestītus, -us, m. *clothing.*
ueto, uetui, uetitum, v. a. 1 *forbid.*
uetus, gen. -eris, *old, worn out.*
uīcīnia, -ae, f. *neighbourhood.*
uicissim, adv. *in turns.*
uideo, uīdi, uīsum, v. a. 2 *see, look to, provide.*
uideor, uīsus sum, v. dep. 2 *seem;* **uidētur**, *it seems good.*
uīlis, -e, *of little worth, cheap.*
uīn = *uīsne.*
uincibilis, -e, *likely to win.*
uinco, uīci, uīctum, v. a. and n. 3 *overcome, prove, win.*
uīnolentus, -a, -um, *in one's cups.*
uir, uiri, m. *man, husband.*
uirgo, -inis, f. *maid, girl.*
uirtus, -ūtis, f. *manly qualities, manliness, valour, virtue.*
uis, acc. uim, f. *violence, quantity.*
uīso, uīsi, uīsum, v. a. 3 *go to see, visit.*
uīta, ae, f. *life, way of life, livelihood.*
uitupero, v. a. 1 *revile.*

uīuo, uīxi, uīctum, v. n. 3 *live*, *am alive.*

uīuos, -a, -om, *alive*, *living.*

uix, adv. *barely*, *scarcely*, *hardly.*

uixdum, adv. *hardly yet.*

ulcīscor, ultus sum, v. dep. 3 *avenge*, *punish.*

ulterior, -us, *further.*

ultimus, -a, -um, *furthest*, *last*, *end of.*

ultro, adv. *actually*, *positively.*

unciātim, adv. *ounce by ounce.*

unde, pron. and adv. rel. and interrog. *from whom*, *from which place*, *from what place*, *from whence.*

unguo, unxi, ūnctum, v. a. 3 *anoint.*

ūnicus, -a, -um, *only.*

ūniuorsus, -a, -um, *whole*, *all together.*

ūnus, -a, -um, *one*, *sole.*

uoco, v. a. 1 *call*, *invite.*

uolo, uolui, uelle, v. n. irreg. *am ready*, *am willing.*

uoltus, -us, m. *face.*

uoluntas, -ātis, f. *will*, *good-will*, *readiness.*

uolup, clipt n. of uolupis used as adv. *according to will*, *satisfactory*, *pleasing.*

uorsūra, -ae, f. *money borrowed to pay a debt.*

uorto, uorti, uorsus sum, v. a. 3 *turn*, *made to turn out.*

uoster, -tra, -trum, *your*, *yours.*

usque, adv. *perpetually*, *continuously.*

ūsus, -us, m. *need.*

ut, adv. and conj. (by which), *how*, *when*, *on condition that*, *as;* also used for *utut.*

uterque, utraque, utrumque, *each of two*, *both.*

ūtibilis, -e, *useful.*

utinam (uti + nam), used before an optative verb to emphasize the wish.

ūtor, ūsus sum, v. dep. 3 *make use of*, *use*, *experience.*

utut, adv. *however.*

uxor, -ōris, f. *wife.*

INDEX

www.ingramcontent.com/pod-product-compliance
Ingram Content Group UK Ltd.
Pitfield, Milton Keynes, MK11 3LW, UK
UKHW020447010325
455719UK00015B/462